JOSEPH

To:
Sue + Bob

From:
Dr. Joseph Blaho Jr

Enjoy Life !!

Manufactured in the United States of America, Canada, or in the United Kingdom when distributed elsewhere.

Joseph – Building Financial Literacy – Increase Your Wealth by 50%

ISBN: Paperback: 978-1-7334077-7-9
ISBN: Hardcover: 978-1-7334077-5-5
ISBN: Kindle: 978-1-7334077-6-2

Library of Congress Control Number: 2019915096

Cover Design: Adobe Images | Angie Anayla
Copyediting: Becky Norwood
Proofreading: Natalie McQueen
Interior layout: Anna Goldsworthy
Published by Spotlight Publishing™
https://www.SpotlightPublishing.Pro

Contact Dr. Joseph Blake Jr:

JOSEPH

Building Financial Literacy
Increase your wealth by 50%

by

Dr. Joseph M. Blake Jr.

Spotlight PUBLISHING

GOODYEAR, AZ

Endorsements

Dr. Blake offers an engaging and comprehensive study of financial decision-making among faithful individuals and organizations. As a long-time experienced Investment Advisor, he asks challenging questions, and offers his unique, experience-based advice to anyone who looks for guidance on how to improve their own financial situation, while being honest to their faith.

Dr. Jelena Vucetic
Author, Entrepreneur, Professor

I commend Dr. Blake for tackling the monumental topic of financial literacy in his book, JOSEPH, Building Financial Literacy. Dr. Blake motivates and encourages one to do some self-examination when it comes to handling finances and then to move from theoretical knowledge to practical know-how and application. His book contains a wealth of information and is long overdue.

Keith C. Pinkard, MBA
Aerospace Science Instructor

Dr. Blake really made his vision on Financial Literacy come to life in a manner that is relatable and palatable to everyone. This book empowers you with the knowledge and wisdom to make a positive difference in ones' life, and the ability to make wiser, more informed decisions no matter what your position in life. An inspiring and refreshing view on how financial literacy and spiritual teachings are all encompassing and not mutually exclusive.

Canisha Current
Author and Financial Advisor

Dedication

This book is dedicated to my Mother Loretta Irene (Ellis) Blake, aka "Minky" who raised me at 915 N. Stricker St. in Baltimore, MD 21217 on the Westside in the Harlem Park Neighborhood. I know for some of you from around the way, you thought it was Mickey, like Mickey mouse but it is Minky like a Mink coat. Momma never sought to correct anyone, she just rolled with it, but for the record, it is "Minky". ☺ Bmore, (Be More Careful) as some affectionately refer our hometown, others may say, "Charm City".

My Mom was the motivating factor driving me toward building a successful life and in being a 'good boy'. My mother was the driving force behind my obtaining my Doctor of Management in Organizational Leadership Degree. My little sister, Coretta P. Blake, obtained a dual Master's in Human Service & Healthcare Administrations.

Before Mom passed away in June 2012, I was able to tell my mother, "Momma, you raised a good man." I am not a perfect man, but you raised a good man Mamma." My Mom answered, "That's all right." And I was satisfied with that.

The findings in this book reflect my dedication to helping people understand personal finance from a different viewpoint, an Educated-Street perspective.

Abstract

The purpose of this book is not to draw out one's financial knowledge. Nor is it to test a person's understanding of financial products. My intent is to help people analyze their economic interests, explore their monetary attitudes, and explain their own money values. A qualitative methodology* allows the most noticeable influences to fully develop and provided an actionable and participatory inquiry with the purpose to solve a social concern.

Direct experience is designed to allow inductive insights to evolve as the participants describe the 'said' discernments and understanding of financial literacy. The people in this case study were adults who have religious affiliations with the organizations in the case study and were willing to assist in the research effort. The NVIVO software was instrumental in the collection and analyzing pertinent data, to develop a model for learning.

The study examined concerns for faith-based organizations seeking to define the influence of religiosity, behavioral economics, and actionable learning pertaining to financial literacy and decision-making. My twenty-five-year experience as an Investment Advisor Representative, personally reading the bible from cover-to-cover eight times and being a student of biblical teachings, heightened my desire to understand how religion influences economic decision-making.

*Qualitative research is defined as a market research method that focuses on obtaining data through open-ended and conversational communication. This method is not only about "what" people think but also "why" they think so.

Contents

Illustrations

Foreword

My name is Dr. Alfred Craig Sr. I was a pastor for 42 years, and in business for over 20 years as owner of 2 hair salons. In those years I had the opportunity of traveling around the world. One of the most precious things my experience and travels afforded me was the opportunity to me great people. Dr. Joe Blake is one of those individuals. I've had the privilege of knowing him as his pastor, his mentor and as a businessman. One thing that has always stood out was his interest in finance and helping others create wealth. If someone informed me that Dr. Blake was writing a book and gave me five seconds to guess what the theme was, I would without hesitation say it is on finance. Being an author of three books myself I understand the power of the pen, as it is a reflection of my passion, my perspective, and who I am as a person.

This is why I believe Dr. Joe Blake being one of the most talented individuals I know, would take the time and do the proper research in order to produce a skillful, carefully written and timely book on Building Financial Literacy. It was his perspective and passion as a person that drove him and helped him press through and overcome the obstacles, setbacks and hindrances that come with producing such an excellent and masterful book.

This book connects us with the relevancy of today's economics, especially as it pertains to religious influences and economic decision-making. Dr. Blake confronts the harsh reality of many people, churches and faith-based organizations who at one time were a vehicle of assistance for their communities but were affected by the crippling monetary structure of our country during the years of 2007 – 2009.

Dr. Blake gives us practical and actionable information that will help us become an active participant in creating a financial future, so that the economic lessons taught from the Bible do not stagnate and stay within the confines of the religious text, but be experienced once we leave our place of worship. This book is not just a novel or a quick read, but a literary work that should be studied and taught to our children, in our schools, our churches and businesses. It provides answers to the perplexing problems facing our families, cities and nation. Many books are being written about money and wealth, but very few really go into detail and not only present the problem, but give us answers that work.

Having known Dr. Joe Blake for over 15 years and watching his life, he's not only giving us theory, but knowledge based on time tested facts that are working in his life.

May you be encouraged and lifted with hope as you read this book, knowing that better days are ahead. You will become competent and knowledgeable in the area of finances. You will acquire skills that many take for granted. Get ready for your future to be improved and your economic wellbeing to be developed. You will be inspired and amazed as you Build Financial Literacy.

Dr. Alfred E. Craig Sr.
Author of Going for Greatness, Spiritual Warfare,
And It's My Destiny to Prosper

Acknowledgments

I want to acknowledge my wife, Corina Blake, who graduated with a BS in Psychology. Her tireless efforts of listening to my philosophical discussion on the influence of financial literacy on faith-based epistemology were instrumental to my success.

I salute the patience of my children, Joe III, Trayvone, Chervonda Blake and Jessica Misquez who endured numerous in-depth conversations about education, economic behaviorism, and religiosity.

By the way! Joe III has a Master's in Information Systems while in pursuit of a PhD in Human Capital Management, Trayvone has a Master's in Information Technology with emphasis in Digital Forensics with honors, 1st Lieutenant Chervonda is pursuing her Master's in Business Administration, and Jessica has a Master's in Social Work.

This book serves as further encouragement for them to continues succeeding in their own life endeavors.

.1.

WHAT WENT DOWN

Everything! Unless you have been hiding under a large rock. Many of us know, that during the years 2007 – 2009, the United States sifted through an economic upheaval of epic proportions nearly crippling the entire monetary structure of the country.

The financial crisis was the most significant occurrence since the Great Depression and did not stop in the United States (US) alone; it spread throughout the globe, and radically changed the viewpoint of the world's financial infrastructure. (Angelides, 2011)

According to Angelides (2011) the conclusion of the matter stemmed from human nature, action, and inaction of the individual as well as societal irresponsibility to account for human weakness. Notice, no one mentioned having the right stock, the highest yielding bond, the hottest real estate market, or any other form of investments. The purpose of my book is to explore the foundational building blocks defining financial literacy and to identify what is necessary to gain a better understanding of the constructs to employ them. Financial literacy is the ability of an individual to gain access to economic information and make use of financial concepts to make effective choices (Servon & Kaestner, 2008).

In the aftermath of the financial crisis, $11 trillion in household wealth has disappeared, and there were more than 26 million people out of work, unemployed, and not being able to find work; some discouraged workers have plainly given up looking for suitable employment. (Angelides, 2011) Typically, in times of crisis those who suffer misfortune seek refuge in nonprofit organizations for assistance, but unfortunately, they too were affected by the financial debacle. (Castaneda, 2004) As a result, the churches that faith-based constituents received assistance from in times of trouble, now face the harsher reality of not being able to assist their religious community. This scenario is not an isolated incident and in fact the financial crisis influenced a broad spectrum of organizations.

This case study revealed that the Bible provides the information necessary to faith-based constituents. Those who believed in these concepts had predetermined financial success in their life. Adherents should not have less than needed to survive or live a life of scarcity; Biblical teachings exclude them from the ramifications arising from this type of crisis. However, this was not the case.

The link between the economic crisis, financial savvy, and faith-based constituents is the connection of these traits to influences on prosperity teachings. Biblical theologians have depicted the lives of iconic religious leaders who obtained wealth, substance, and abundance. For example, Job had much substance, Job 1:3 (KJV), and Solomon possessed great abundance, 2nd Chron 1:12 (KJV), Abraham was rich, Gen. 13:12 (KJV) and all were men who believed in one creator of the universe. Faith-based educational endeavors foretell of a time when the wealth of the sinners is set aside or given to those proven by living a religious lifestyle. Prov. 13:22 (KJV) This is a predetermined spiritual theory needing a tangible connection or means to access financial information to make use of its concept.

> "But there is ample evidence that those who learn how to achieve access to the bath of knowledge that already envelops the world will be the future's aristocrats of achievement, and that they will be far more numerous than any aristocracy in history."

> (Presidential Committee on Information Literacy: Final Report, 1989, p. 3)

Accessing financial knowledge can be expensive and there are members of the faith-based institutions who do not have the monetary resources to obtain this knowledge. Adherents believe there will be a time when wealth would be given to them, and therefore there is a need to position themselves to capture the influx of an economic windfall. Job 27:16-17 (KJV)

Stric...

Did you take ... of you? In life, ... fundamenta... is no room... sister, "Thi... reference. Step ... on. When the price o... a nosedive, that meant it w... other one of the greatest fire sa...

When I was a kid, my momma wo... town Baltimore on Howard Street, or up... shop for clothing. Easter shopping was a 'sore s... mom would buy me one outfit, BUT my sister wou... outfits. Momma would say, "Little Joe," girls clothing is ... boys clothing. I can get Sweetie (my sister) two or three outfi... same cost as one outfit for you.

$%@#$, I knew momma loved Sweetie more than me. My momma would put some money aside, so we could have good clothes on Easter. Despite being on welfare and later earning meager wages, my mother made things happen.

Peeking back to when I was a child, and seeing forward as an adult, it means that those who held a significant cash position and were in the right place, at the right time, capitalized on real-time opportunity. My mother did not use credit, she used cash to pay for things. The best financial place to be in, when prices dropped to historic lows, is in a cash position, and in the place to buy things up. Being in debt does not help this cause.

, facing religious leaders pertains to the
.1.-based learners have of secular financial
, Faith-based learners, for the purposes of this
nstituents who ascribe to religious teachings
:ir implications on living an abundant lifestyle.
have illustrated in religious texts lessons about
stament religious leaders who obtained substance,
riches/wealth. The Bible describes the patriarch Job
substance and there is a detail illustration of what his
.tained. (Job 1:3, KJV)
Jmon of Israel possessed great abundance and wisdom.
.12 KJV) The story of Abraham discussed in Genesis 13:2 ex-
at he was very rich, and it depict his riches as cattle, silver,
.1. These were men who believed in one creator of the universe.
based teachings also speak of a scripture that says that one day
wealth of the sinful, or believers who miss the Godly behavior mark,
.ll have their wealth given to those that are doing right in the eyes of
God. (Prov. 13:22 KJV).

These premises are attributed as a spiritual matter, however, there
is a tangible need for the scriptures to provide explicit instructions on
how to access financial information to make use of its concept in its
natural state. Research has illustrated the benefits to those who learn
how to achieve access to a plethora of financial information and knowledge; such persons will become future philanthropists. (Presidential
Committee on Information Literacy: Final Report, 1989, p. 3) Gaining
access to financial information costs money, and there are members
of the faith-based institutions who lack the resources to access the
proper technological tools or, have the wherewithal to use them. Faith-
based constituents declare that now is the time for an inductive plan,
positioning them to capture the essence of an economic windfall. (Job
27:16-17, KJV)

The Bible gives constituents a background, rationale, and examples
that form a presumed blueprint, and serves as a model on how wealth is
accumulated. On the other hand, in the current state or resultant situation, faith-based constituents have not found themselves in a positive

money position. 90% of church members are in some form of debt and rely on faith or religion to guide their everyday activities, including financial literacy. (Wolgemuth, 2008; Harris, 2001) Depending on one's faith is predictable; however, there is an actionable component of faith that requires constituents to become active participants in creating a financial future.

Faith-based supporters anchored their knowledge in the belief that by being a good steward of money through giving tithes and offerings, they would receive a just reward. (Nonaka & Nishiguchi, 2001, p. 13) This case study's resolve was to inquire how economic lessons taught from the Bible materialize in an adherent's life. Its intent was to explain how the lessons could possibly stagnant, staying within the confines of the religious text and not experienced by believers, once they leave their place of worship. Bottomline, the study was meant to describe how the information gleaned from teaching does or does not correlate into today's language to the degree that it causes or influences one to recreate the learning process, outside of the arena in which the lessons were originally taught.

The key is to delve into the lived experiences of the people who desire the key behavioral trait necessary to translate knowledge from the Bible into a vibrant lived reality. *"Education needs a new model of learning-learning that is based on the informational resources of the real world and learning that is active and integrative, not passive and fragmented."*
(Presidential Committee on Information Literacy: Final Report, 1989)

Believers who can understand secular financial language to the extent that they are able to anchor monetary principles into action are uncertain. (Nonaka & Nishiguchi, 2001, pg. 13) The scriptures indicate that Christians need to achieve financial literacy for five fundamental premises:

1. To validate the testimony of the scriptures.
   3rd John 2:1(KJV)
2. Become a platform of influence.
   Psalm 1:1-3 (KJV)

3. Provide resources for expansion.
   Duet. 8:18
4. When in a negative state one cannot be of benefit to themselves or others, and
5. To realize its already provided or purchased.
   2nd Cor 8:9 (KJV)

If it is not clear how other religious organizations introduced in this study perceive their economic role, one of the aims of this case study was to explore the spiritual premises of fiscal beliefs.

It is essential for constituents of faith to have financial literacy, especially those from minority groups that are more likely to be misled or taken advantage of in a financial transaction. (Gerardi & Willen, 2008) According to Servon and Kaestner (2008), financial literacy refers to the ability of the individual to understand how to gain access to economic information and make use of financial concepts. The fallout from the current economic recession reveals that irregular home mortgage loans were made to minorities at an alarming rate. As a result, minority owned homes by African Americans and Latino homeowners grew from 27% in 2002 to 36% of interracial sales accounting for 74% of subprime sales between 1990 and 2002.

That affects this segment of society more so than any other ethnic groups. (Gerardi & Willen, 2008) A fundamental approach and shift in the thought process for minorities needs to occur regarding traditional banking and financial intelligence. There is a need for an initiative that stimulates an experienced-based learning process which the individual may appreciate the need for controlling their economic future. (Estelami, 2009)

Another equally challenging dilemma is the understanding of the computer banking system which by African American and Hispanics are at the opposite end of understanding the digital divide, thus the online banking community has also alienated the same two ethnic groups. (Estelami, 2009) This case study notes that the literature pieces depict a gap in the knowledge obtained and indicates that there are no tangible influences to remedy the challenges these groups face.

The phenomenological or direct experience case study may provide insight into the trends of how the knowledge about money is acquired, articulated, and employed by faith-based constituents. To promote economic independence and improve one's quality of existence, there is a lifelong need to know relevant and up-to-date information.
(Presidential Committee on Information Literacy: Final Report, 1989)

Religious principles may alter or change the viewpoint pertaining to financial illiteracy, resulting in unrealized goals and objectives. Learning models along with having access to data and resources to make the necessary adjustments to acquire monetary substance need to be revolutionized. Financial education needs an innovative model of learning, learning that encompasses common and non-common subject matter that actively engages the learner to recreate principles outside of the realm in which is a learning environment.
(Presidential Committee on Information Literacy: Final Report, 1989)

The competitive nature of financial marketing, with the argument of fee-based versus commission advice or internet-based learning, confound the matter. The disparate nature of gaining viable access to financial knowledge becomes caught in a quagmire between entities whose sole intent is to increase organizational profits inadvertently at the expense of the individual. The nonprofit industry becomes the initial organization to address middle to lower income families about their financial matters. American people who are religious turn to matters of faith to ease the difficult challenges faced during times of upheaval and uncertainty. (Ladd, 1987). This study addresses matters pertinent to religious organizations with the proper motivation that could increase its aid, along with the professional services they provide to constituents. (Kissane, 2007)

The research efforts described the behaviors believed to have influenced the gap in knowledge that can be attributed to the teaching methods of financial educators on, and how the information can be incorporated into the lives of people. Also, there were no structural programs, no common teaching curriculum that the federal government offers, as to how one can become financially literate. This lack of economic adroit actions or inactions could be identifiers as to the trigger of the financial crisis of 2008 – 2009. (Angelides, 2011)

Now, the Federal Reserve's personal financial education initiatives highlight the role of economic education in financial institutions, the community, and faith-based groups. (Education, 2004) Theoretical ideologies, routine progress, and menial involvement in the obtaining of the necessary knowledge are a crucial root cause to this problem.

> "...three themes shape its history in education: philosophical ideas, procedural developments, along with participatory and advocacy practices."

(Creswell, 2005, p. 41)

Educational learning models must contain theory and its relevant empirical equivalent to measure, change, and increase financial literacy traits. Researchers probe into study efforts primarily from a theoretical perspective reinforced with empirical evidence.

A theoretical approach researcher favors constrictive precepts that support a presumed theory or its plausible causes. In doing so, observing the constrictive precepts are ineffective in causing change within people to increase their desires to want to learn, understand, and know what it means to be financially literate. This is because constituents already have notions or precepts about the money they have, or want to acquire, this 'said' understanding needs to be illuminated or brought to light.

A qualitative research approach explores the feelings, emotions and thoughts of constituents, providing rich insight into the problem. The resolve emerges from the participant to the researcher, versus the researcher defining a probable meaning of a problem. An empirical approach researcher converts the precepts to testable hypotheses, and the researcher can introduce traits. (Cooper & Schindler, 2003) The endeavor illustrated, described, and explained the best plausible means to state or address the inherent challenges of constituents based on the members interview discussion. The case study intended to describe the economic interest of participants regarding their financial decision-making. It illustrated the attitudes held by participants toward the economic environment, and perceptions regarding choices to take advantage of financial opportunities. It explained the values held, and behaviors exhibited towards achieving a sustainable level of economic acceptance.

What is the Problem?

The general problem is that there is a gap between faith-based theory of knowledge and the influence of financial literacy based on cognitive behaviors. (Harris, 2001) The faith-based community's teleological (predetermined outcome) monetary advantage collapsed along with the ongoing financial crisis. (Neuman, 2003, p. 158) Religious doctrine has not prevailed any better than those of non-faith during the economic recession, as many congregational members with 2,350 Bible verses discussed the topic of money while being in some form of bondage to debt. (Harris, 2001; Wolgermuth, 2008)

Churches are a viable source for adherents to turn to when tough times come, however, those safe homes are now facing their own harsh economic reality. In fact, banks foreclosed on 200 religious' institutions in 2008, whereas only 8 suffered this demise eight years earlier, and virtually none a decade prior. (The Wall Street Journal, 2011) According to Servon and Kaestner (2008), financial literacy refers to the ability of the individual to understand how to gain access to economic information and make use of financial concepts.

The consequences for lacking the academic skills in financial matters, can have an unfavorable effect on the efficiency of cohorts and constituents as well as the future of a corporation's productivity. (Drucker, 2008) Mainstream financial literacy collides with religious beliefs, as the ambiguity between spiritual values concerning prosperity is at odds with, and difficult to adhere to, during uncertain economic uncertainty.

Religious philosophical constructs could impede common sense and conflict with one's ability to accumulate capital and could adversely affect the future of a nonprofit corporation by reducing the ability of its constituents to tithe or live a quality lifestyle. (Harris, 2001) This phenomenological or direct experience study explores how faith-based services can define their knowledge of economics and increase its means of providing access to financial information literacy perceived by parishioners.

This was accomplished by randomly interviewing 30 members from three ethnically different religious organizations in the Phoenix Metropolitan Area. The results of this study enabled leaders to further educate ministry scholars, produce financial independence, and to further broaden the matters of canon spirituality. The study identified participatory elements necessary to acquire monetary substance in which abundance and wealth are nonexistent in practical discourse.

The direct experience method identified patterns that could increase the clarity in describing the financial literacy of participants. In describing the financial literacy, the aim improves the adherent's quality of life through better choices in selecting financial products and services, as well as to increase tithing to the respective churches. The results from interviews provided vital insights into economic patterns of faith-based constituents.

Leadership could then distinguish which components to infuse into an actionable, or practical learning model to produce tangible financial insight and results. In determining the theme or patterns of economic behaviors, leaders can further determine what influences are preventing or succeeding in the lives of its constituents. This approach helped establish the necessary level of services needed, and the amount of effort required, to ensure it is successful. (Belcher & DeForge, 2007)

The Reason Why We Are Here

The purpose of the proposed qualitative case study is to describe, explain, and inquire into the financial knowledge of 30 constituents from three different local ministries in Phoenix, Arizona. (Wuthnow, 2002) This case study employed a direct experience designed to explore, as well as describe, the comprehension of personal finance and to answer the question; does religious teachings on prosperity equate to financial literacy to the degree its constituents can obtain and sustain wealth. (Estelami, 2009)

The case study interviewed participants from three different religious establishments in Phoenix, Arizona selected at random to conduct an in-depth interview regarding their experience with faith-based teachings and financial literacy. The participants encompassed three variations of religious disciplines of faith that comprise Christian beliefs. The personal interview is a vibrant resource for illuminative information of the phenomenon aimed at gathering 'said' insight from the lived experiences of the individual. This case study inquired how economic behaviors and cognitive psychology imply suboptimal financial decisions limiting the financially naïve believer, and frequently exhibited by even the most financially educated theologian. (Estelami, 2009)

The tangible relationships or experiences of participants, who have learned to handle financial matters efficiently, may be transferred into practices that others can emulate. Participants, who have learned and achieve the knowledge to access the surfeit of financial knowledge, will become the philanthropist in this new era. (Presidential Committee on Information Literacy: Final Report, 1989)

The resources to obtain the information become a non-issue as constituents acquire monetary resources to further their quest of financial literacy. To increase financial literacy by 50% requires research to determine at what level members have retained money awareness and recommend a course of action to make the goal a reality.

The ability to obtain wealth, and in turn give tithes and offerings in support of religious principles, is the ultimate objective of a faith-based constituent. Deut. 8:18 (KJV) Conflicting arguments exist between the faith-based believers and secular societal viewpoints on the purpose of giving. The bottom-line for faith-based constituents is the acceptance that giving is a lifestyle to maintain as a cheerful reminder of the blessings one receives from God. Therefore, the lack of financial astuteness impedes the ability to fulfill intrinsic worth and value to one's faith.

The George W. Bush administration noted the significant contributions of nonprofit organizations by stating,

"Charity and faith-based groups fulfill the needs of people that no welfare system, no matter how well designed, can possibly fill...in times of personal crisis, people do not need the rules of a bureaucracy; they need the help of a neighbor."

(Wuthnow, 2004, p. 1)

The importance of a faith-based organizational leader's ability to provide and understand the nature of the vital role played out in the financial lives of constituents is greater now, than ever before.

The Research Method

The nature of this study focused on a direct experience designed to identify the logical significance and performance understood by contributors. A typical direct experience research design involves interviewing constituents, giving them the opportunity to express, describe or explain their feelings and emotions. (Yin, 2009) A direct experience case study approach allowed the researcher to observe which traits are pertinent to financial literacy and emulated the current understanding of participants. Participants could speak candidly about the information they have, or the knowledge they have obtained in specified economic subject areas. The information provided by participants emerged into a model of learning that others can use to acquire financial understanding to such a degree that it created actionable financial knowledge.

A participant engaging in an interactive and inquisitive learning process that encourages query, description, and explanation of their conceptualization of economic precepts, learn new information. These precepts can evaluate and contrast against the religious text equivalent and discusses a further understanding of how a participant's view of financial literacy influences by their faith along with the comprehension of other constituents.

The objective assessed what was important to a participant economically and in turn, what actions had they taken thus far to achieve pertinent goals. Then, the effects of additional information assimilated into knowledge gained or retained with an acceptable margin of error as unavoidable or unnoticed. During a 45-minute discussion, the ideas illuminated phenomena of traits inherent in their lifestyle as perceived by the participants in the case study.

The Design Realness

This is a descriptive approach of various economic aspects used to depict consumer logic of behavioral choices regarding the utilization and benefits of a product or service. Participants were given the freedom to express their thinking on what they believe is important economically, and what they perceived was necessary to help them put any new information into practice. This provided the research with the ability to identify a pattern of thinking or, descriptive relationships that can further add solid credence to the importance of this research effort.

A viable measure of predictability from this methodology intentionally added value to research and observation procedures. As the analysis of the data occurred during the gathering of verbal responses, the measures were accumulated. The answers to this problem, can provide church leaders with the attributes necessary to increase the financial skills and awareness of their members who in turn, are able to give more to the organization financially. This could result in an increase in organizational revenue and donations relevant to corporate growth. The members are endowed with the personal finances to fulfill personal, as well as corporate goals and objectives. One conceivable objective could guide constituents into leading a well-balanced lifestyle of wealth, substance, and abundance at the level described as experienced by iconic leaders' in their religious text.

Investigative Questionnaire

The proposed study described the answers to research assumptions that dominated the thoughts of participants and explored pertinent factors that influence their economic behaviors. The inquiry process was constructed to capture the necessary explanation and illuminated the descriptive nature of the behaviors affecting financial literacy's influence. The contrivance allowed for the explorative discussion of participants who appear to have identifiable traits of the logical significance concerning an economic precept.

The second part of the inquiry process explored any identifiable traits of the logical progression or the actionable application of the financial concepts. (Argyris, 1996) The study described how, and if, participants are aware of their economic behaviors and, if they can or are able to make changes in their situation.

1. What are the sentiments that influence financial literacy, and its effects on recreating economic success after learning about monetary principles?
2. How does one transfer teachings on religious prosperity to the knowledge of choosing financial products and services by a group who is unknowingly self-constricted by religious impediments?
3. Do faith-based constituents who discern religious doctrine of wealth know fundamental principles of financial literacy?
4. How important is it that faith-based constituents, who discern religious doctrine of wealth, know fundamental principles of financial literacy?
5. Do faith-based believers who understand religious doctrine about building wealth, exhibit behaviors that do not result in economic actions that relate to financial literacy?
6. How significant is it that faith-based constituents who discern religious doctrine of wealth, know, and exhibit religiosity resulting in economic behaviors that relate to financial literacy?

Participant Standing

The participants are adult learners that are employed on a full-time basis and were randomly chosen or volunteered for the discussion involving financial matters. The typical participant was married, aged between 25-45 years, had children, and their income was above the poverty level. (US Census Bureau, 2011) The acquisition of such information or knowledge could prove to be of immeasurable value to an individual's economic future. This method of selection ensures that those who participate can do so, with no intent for personal gain. This made it certain that the integrity of the research effort and provided rich data during the interviewing sessions. To improve the financial literacy of mature constituents is an intriguing challenge: adults typically do not attend school, in proportion to younger workers, and tend not to have an interest in generic financial literacy classes.

(Servon & Kaestner, 2008)

Behavioral Traits

The traits observed included exploring how financial literacy is important in four basic facets of being a well-informed, well-educated consumer. Consumers can make improved decisions for their families and improve personal economic security and well-being; as well as give to vital and thriving communities, by promoting community economic development. (Mimbs-Johnson & Lewis, 2009) Theoretical results from these traits provided credible discoveries to assist the faith-based leadership with a direction to guide its constituents. The best means to identify the traits came from allowing individuals to control the amount and timing of information given by each participant. (Neuman, 2003) The behavioral traits illustrated by each of the participants during the inquiry efforts, and the choices participants explained as the dialogue unfolds were the basis of economic informational necessary to affect change.

During the research, endeavors identified the phenomena and other traits worthy of noting as the study progressed. The identification of the self-interest of people as the driving mechanisms to acquiring their desires, and when these desires are at an imbalance, trouble loomed. According to Stucke (2010), an individual with a desire for self-interest seeks out, while those that are unusually fair constituents, are forced out, or avoided conflict in an organization. The behavior people exhibit has more to do with what they think is fair and equitable, and the desire to achieve financial independence is a fair assumption. These instances, as in boycotting, where people would withhold their own gratification to address or express a certain collective concern. (Stucke, 2010) Obtaining financial solvency is the pursuit of a vast number of people groups, including faith-based constituents.

The Theory Frame

This research effort was theoretically formulated between three main bodies of interest within the context of management, and organizational leadership in the nonprofit industry. The constituent who seeks to obtain financial knowledge, was at the core of the research effort. The financial industry was important to getting the proper information to those who may need the insight. Leadership holds the key to unlocking the potential of their constituents, and when this is done properly, productivity increases, and the corporation is profitable. This study encompassed organizational learning and how or what financial knowledge to create for constituent. The flow of financial information occurred as the influx of messages came in, and this new information became knowledge when it was anchored in beliefs.

(Nonaka & Nishiguchi, 2001, p. 13)

The financial messages coming into the organization for constituents to accept were not received, because they did not line up with biblical truths. The term Usury in religious text is meant to illustrate the banking system of that day; in those times the perception meant safety or implied security. While in today's technologically advanced banking system, minority groups do not perceive them as safe nor secure, especially because lending institutions prey upon their lack of understanding. (Estelami, 2009) This could infuse the possibility that the usury or banking system is not seeking after the benefit of the account holder, but for its own self-interest as an entity or corporate leadership. (Estelami, 2009)

Over the past decade, debt increased $963 billion, which is a 25% increase from the prior period and banks received $15 billion in penalty fees from consumers in the United States. (Stucke M. E., 2009) This condition is indicative of one or two conclusions, either the consumer is spending far beyond their means, or depositors are gravely miscalculating account balances. Alternatively, monetary institutions are aggressively eager to reap an extensive amount of revenue from its depositors without their prior approval. However, the total of any organization is the combined efforts of its constituents, therefore, when self-interested individuals seek after profits for the company, the ill-advised efforts may come at the expense of society as whole, or could signal a need to financially educate the consumer.

The study also explored identifying factors that led to the role self-interest holds on the perceptions of financial literacy and, how it coincides with human action or inaction. The illogical or immoderate desires of self-interested parties have free reign within a capitalistic structure that lacks moral turpitude. This inadvertently renders well-intended financial advice ineffective on a broad scale, before signs acknowledged by notable economic professionals. (Angelides, 2011)

The illicit financial behaviors exhibited by individuals in upper echelon positions of corporations proves the need to address leadership traits and their potential influences on organizational outcomes. (White & Lean, 2008) Responsible leadership accounts for actions deemed reprehensible or detrimental to the corporations' existence whether it is intentional or accidental. This study described a model of ethical economic leader behavior resultant to discoveries offered during the interview process. (White & Lean, 2008) Constituents closer to the potential mayhem can provide a detail description of what was seen from a ground-floor reference not typically realized as an advantage point.

Two terms identified or referenced the espoused values of adherents who ascribe to faith-based sentiments. One such term is 'God's Plan' also known as teleology. This term describes the spiritual belief of one's circumstances attributed to a predetermined outcome that must happen because it is desired or deserved from one's creator. (Neuman, 2003, p. 158) The other term is religiosity, which describes the frequency of an individual's behaviors involving church activities (Lehrer, 2004).

Summary

In the next chapter, the literature review scholarly explains the reasons for this research endeavor. The foundational articles as well as current discoveries regarding the topic credits the need for a financial literacy renewal within the lives of people. Corporate and individual economic behaviors nearly crippled the globe, and the volatile market activity, when seen in the past, is not healthy or sustainable. The nonprofit industry befriends people and fellow organizations with their desires to help the common man in times of uncertainty. This literature review illustrates the complexity of financial dexterity and its necessity in the lives of constituents.

DR BLAKE'OLOGY

So, should I avoid sin (yes, at all cost) or attend church more often (you better)? Which move should I make, what skill do I need to learn, or ability to acquire that leads to a wealthier lifestyle?

I once heard a Pastor say that we/I should not put spiritual scriptures to worldly things. **Word!** In John 1:1-3, God says that in the beginning all things were made by him and without him nothing was made.

All financial system, money concepts, and spending programs were already made by God. We need to find out what they are, understand them, and use them to our advantage.

.2.

WHAT I READ ABOUT IT

WHILE in chapter 1 we provided an overview and background of the study with future implications to researchers and illustrated the topic of interest, the background of the problem, the problem statement, nature of the study, purpose of the study, and research questions. Furthermore, we showcased how to direct experience aspects were established, participant status discussed, along with traits pertinent to the research were addressed.

Now, in chapter 2 we examine the literary review of germinal literature expounding financial literacy, faith-based epistemology, and behavioral economics to describe the constituent's actions to learning key financial concepts influencing the inquiry of lessons learned. The content of the foundational work began in the early 50's and reflects the attitudes of that time that lacked ethnic or religious censorship and sensitivity. Although this research may depict a stereotypical illustration of certain religious groups, its discoveries are significant to the study, in providing a link between religion and money.

Title Searches, Articles, Research Documents, and Journals

In this literature review, articles and studies came from peer-reviewed scholarly journals; germinal text; dissertations and thesis; as well as resources obtained from the library at the University of Phoenix. The use of some non-peer-reviewed material was necessary to provide a current perspective of the financial crisis in the United States, as well as the World it continues to distance itself from. Professional literature from organizations serving economic behaviors, religion, and business was necessary to fully understand the depth of issues regarding Financial Literacy. Table 1 below illustrates a breakdown of the types of resources used.

Stricker Street Story

My Godparents Mr. Oscar and Elizabeth Lynn (RIP), lived right around the corner on Mosher St. I would often walk by their house with a frown on my face on my way to the barbershop. Mr. Oscar would say, "What's wrong Bo Pete?" (Ok, everyone has a nickname). I would respond, "I got to get a haircut". Mr. Oscar would say, "It will be alright!"

One day, I was tasked with spending the weekend with Mr. Oscar, because Ms. Elizabeth was having surgery. I was to be a big boy and run for help if needed. So, my Mom packed me a weekend bag and I hopped around the corner to Mr. Oscars neighborhood. He had all the right vitals for a kid including two cases of "Pineapple" soda pop! He said, "Bo Pete" you can have what you want! I was in heaven. Now, Mr. Oscar and Ms. Elizabeth were avid churchgoers and would take me and sweetie (my sister) to Shiloh Baptist Church on Freemont Ave.

The next day, I heard this loud talking coming from the dining room area. Peering through the banisters leading upstairs, I could see Mr. Oscar sitting at the table, with his wooden leg standing beside him, and reading this big ole book. Then I would hear him say, "The Lord said...." not sure what came afterwards. I thought to myself, yea "this dude has lost it" and I would bebop into the kitchen and grab another "Pineapple" soda pop to finish watching 'Captain Chesapeake' on Channel 45.

This weekend sparked three things in my life: 1. My love for Pineapple soda 2. A desire to read (especially the word of God) 3. My mom had the right influencers in my life.

My point is, read the Word! Not just this book or that book, read the entire Bible. I challenge you to read from Genesis to Revelations.

Table 1

Literature Review Source

Key Word Searched	Peer Reviews Searched	Popular Works	Germinal Works	Books	Studies
Leadership Significance		5		10	
Literacy	25	2	5		
Financial Literacy	12	3			3
Financial Management, Wealth and Religion	27	2			
Self-Efficacy	6				
Personal Finance					
Theologians/Faith-Based	10				
Quality Training/Team-work	9	1	7		
Methodologies/Survey's	8				
Direct Experience	2		2		1
Learning Theories	1				
Strategy	4				
Effectiveness	1				
Organizational Development	6	1			
Total Reviewed 153	111	14	14	10	4

Much of the scholarly writing and germinal research related to literacy and financial management, wealth, and religion. A cross selection of 80 solid resources were used to build this study and solidified the findings in an annotated bibliography (see Appendix C). The competencies of the studies were between 2003 and 2011, and one study was conducted five decades prior. However, most of the literature review comes from resources within in a five-year period, with one of the foundational texts and research within four years of the review influencing the direction of the analysis.

Boulding (1952) laid the foundation for exploring the influence of economic factors resulting from religious instruction. The way in which people believe and accumulate wealth is a byproduct of their religious practices. (Boulding, 1952) Thoughts of economic influences during this industrial period differ from current thinking on precepts surround financial matters. Some religious groups pursue intellectual capital as the means, the thoughts and the actions to reach levels of wealth.

According to Boulding (1952), the Jewish culture emphasized gaining intellectual capital as a prelude to actuate economic success. Notably, the Jewish community is known for its ability to gain an economic edge on other religious groups. At the opposite side of religious thinking and economic status is the conservative Protestant, who centers his or her foundation for security in building and strengthening the family unit. (Boulding, 1952) Moderate Protestants and Catholics are at the middle of this continuum, and these groups tend to accumulate a moderate amount of capital with an average sized family unit. During the 1950s the number of religious groups in operation on a national level was limited, and pale in comparison to the religious groups existing during this study.

Boulding (1952) illustrates the Protestant thinking of avoiding 'sin' which is defined as loose living, being indifferent, slothfulness, and dishonesty; seen as detrimental to yielding spiritual insights to accumulate wealth. Living and exhibiting the appropriate behaviors as what is right as an individual experiences' life is an example. The Christian believer uses the example to capitalize on the opportunity to accumulate skills commensurate with success. In the process of an individual becoming wealthy, the society in turn becomes wealthy as the individual can offer less fortunate individuals (Boulding, 1952).

The way societies views have a large influence on the economy and religiosity sways a family's resolve for economic understanding (Lehrer, 2004). The current thinking on religion differs from those depicted in Boulding (1952) whose research illustrates four main religious grouping Jews, Catholics, conservative, and moderate Protestants. Wherein Boulding (1952) approaches were to avoid sin, Lehrer (2004) emphasized involvement in religious activities as a prelude to achieving economic success. In addition to the main religious entities, today's modern religious groups compound a diverse thinking on religion where Mormon, Muslim, non-denominational and inter-denominational beliefs permeate the nation and have gained cultural acceptance.

Lehrer (2004) introduces the concept of religiosity as it infuses the influence of active involvement in religious activities constituents contribute to as an act of religious reverence. The amount of active involvement in Sunday attendance, mid-week learning sessions, participation in ancillary programs all add to accumulating intellectual capital for parishioners.

Lewis (2009) described in a study, four types of traits used in practical reasoning and includes context, valued ends, means, and consequences as descriptive efforts. Furthermore, the study explored the mental accounting phenomenon, which was how individuals tend to view money, as a function of the source of funds or where it intends to be spent. (Estelami, 2009)

The construction of the study-identified precepts expressed based on detailed descriptions of a participant's experience of mental accounting and hyperbolic discounting responses to research questions. Mental accounting merely places monetary expenditures into proverbial 'bucks' or 'envelopes' as prescribed methods of spending funds in a habitual fashion. Accordingly, mental accounting is the set of cognitive operations used by individuals and households to organize, evaluate, and keep track of financial activities. (Thaler, 1999, p. 183)

This involves choosing how outcomes are perceived, assigning of activities to accounts and the evaluation of those accounts. Hyperbolic discounting centers on the time value of money, where money received today had more value than money received tomorrow. (Estelami, 2009) The information collected on the behavioral traits and relationships described and derived from the action's participants had taken toward economic dexterity. One of the primary goals was to deprogram consumer's decision-making style and increase the desire for accumulating wealth versus consuming assets given the information revealed. To accomplish the goal, anchor-based decision-making concept were initiated and recommended that financial concepts should be taught to individuals when they are young. (Estelami, 2009)

In hyperbolic discounting, as the time of obtaining a goal increases or is further away, the value assigned to the specific action diminishes in importance to the constituent. For example, speaking to a young potential investor about retirement planning, surprisingly does not truly hold value in their eyes. The reason this occurs, stems from the precept that this type of a long-term goal is too far away for them to consider thinking about it, so they choose not to plan. In hyperbolic discounting equations, the relative decline in value decreases as a delay in obtaining a gain increase. (Yi, Gatchalian, & Bickel, 2006)

American consumerism contradicts the ability to wait to build or obtain wealth, as well as being patient to achieve equitable results. One interesting phenomenon in financial and economic research is the linkage of current monetary concerns to the misfortunes of the Great Depression. (Grebler, 1986) The adversity of the most challenging economic decline in United States history has earmarked itself as the benchmark for any monetary upheaval. Consumers relive the times of the great depression in detail, until the times like those have inevitably returned to plague them and to cause them to live in turmoil.

The plethora of information on financial matters during the economic depression era of 2007 - 2009 proved valuable to substantiating and understanding the totality of financial literacy. A broader implication for financially literate leaders is evident as corporations around the nation and globe faced economic challenges of epic proportions. The need exists for new leadership in the corporate monetary arena and a call for change in the economic paradigm of society. It is time to inform, educate, and inspire faith-based constituents with the goal of improving this population's preparedness for change because of the financial services bill H.R. 4173: Restoring American Financial Stability Act of 2010.

The literature review identifies historical and current literature relating to the cognitive behaviors regarding faith-based constituents desire of obtaining financial dexterity. The literature review examines actionable knowledge measures that would be pertinent to leaders to develop a design or create situations and environments for the learner to be original in thought-producing what we claim to have high external validity. (Fulmer & Keys, 2008)

The concept of actionable financial knowledge derives its core value from the fundamentals of model II learning where theory fuses into a useful existence. Whereas Model 1 learning would only correct errors or flaws in a system, but does nothing to facilitate learning. Model II learning concepts culminate in four distinct areas of research deemed necessary to empirically suit the research questions designed for this study. (Argyris, 1996) The areas of focus are (a) Historical overview and current findings, (b) Financial Literacy, (c) Faith-based Epistemology and (d) Behavioral Economics.

Historical Overview and Current Findings

The historical underpinning of the literature included in the review provided insight into the interest in the correlation between religion and money. Boulding (1952) initiated the approach with an inquiry designed to discover elements that improve the financial status of certain religious groups. As the resolve to determine the nature of man and society sought to expand, faith and finance are at the core of this understanding. The current research conducted by Lehrer (2008) moves the intrigue on this subject matter into its present state. The 56-year time span, from between 1952 and 2008 between the two studies illustrate an interesting quagmire for leaders, especially in the nonprofit industry.

This lost research time could indicate the gap in the missing financial learning by a generation that resulted in a generation that repeated behaviors resembling the Great Depression. However, these actions not only gripped the United States, but also reached around the globe to cripple economies of foreign nations. Millions of families lost their homes during the financial crisis, drastically changing the quality of life for those who were victimized by misguided organizations during the economic calamity. (Angelides, 2011)

Organizations need active and appreciative learning cultures that introduce financial educational initiatives, enacting a social responsibility to ensure constituent monetary understandings. (Barrett & Peterson, 2000) Despite society moving into a knowledge-based economy, the rule of financial literacy still appears evasive. Drucker (2008) emphasizes the importance of the knowledge worker, and if one were a knowledge worker, self-interest would drive them to find the answer to their economic woes.

Certain rules govern what one's habitual behaviors influence and what constituents accept as financial literacy, mental accounting or hyperbolic discounting. (Thaler, 2008) Consumer choice is driven by emotional concerns more so than rational decision-making or pure common sense. When these choices are rooted in religious beliefs, the probability of disturbing one's comfort zone becomes improbable or irrelevant.

Financial Literacy

The goal is to improve financial literacy by helping others to understand the technological changes affecting the financial sector. The literatures in the study has one centralized theme that permeates its discoveries, to understand financial literacy is to gain technological understanding. (Servon & Kaestner, 2008)

Comprehension of financial matters is crucial to safeguarding the discoveries of cohorts and constituents. Today, consumption of goods and services exceed the preservation of capital for future use and the public is unaware. The national debt continues to escalate at an alarming rate, while organizational, governmental, and personal budgets cannot balance themselves. (Presidential Committee on Information Literacy: Final Report, 1989) Thaler (1999) noted the satisfaction, or the concept of transaction utility, as a key to understanding the economic puzzle.

The political makeup of some organizations and certain components of corporate cultures, chose injustice over fair dealings to sooth the bottom-line (Andrews & Kacmer, 2001). Family values eroded and

WHAT I READ ABOUT IT

middle-class Americans discounted the possibility of a society with the ability to heal its financial woes. Amid the turmoil is the religious, non-profit industry that typically establishes programs to reach out to those in need. The irony is that nonprofit organizations at the time needed a handout to keep themselves profitable (Castaneda, 2004). When the needs of parishioners cannot be met, the truth then becomes an illusion, as corporation and the thoughts of justice create doubt in the minds of the people.

Corporations comprise the sum of the efforts of hundreds and thousands of individual actors who contribute to a whole system that appears anemic. Mental budgets evade or give into suboptimal financial choices that typically forgo rational behaviors. (Estelami, 2009) No clear indicators direct constituents to entities to receive information and knowledge necessary to conquer the overwhelming financial data available. As the inability of households to save has eroded the moral fiber of a positive financial consciousness, the phenomenon continues to evade comprehension. The role of self-interest and competition appear as fuel toward a future destiny creating a battle for financial supremacy. (Stucke, 2009)

DR BLAKE'OLOGY

epistemology | noun

The theory of knowledge, especially regarding its methods, validity, and scope. Epistemology is the investigation of what distinguishes justified belief from opinion.

Faith-Based Epistemology or Theory of Knowledge

Constituent's belief in spiritual matters anchor spiritual knowledge with religious doctrine, enriched with economic premonitions. Religion and money are in some instances a volatile mixture in an interesting phenomenon. Identifying thoughts guided by a value system with an empirical connection can point toward a successful affiliation based on the appropriate. (Barro & McCleary, 2003) The need to spiritually connect religious text instructions to the successful accumulation of wealth then becomes of utmost concern. The effect wealth has on an individual then should be measurable and the amount necessary to repeat the occurrences should heighten leadership's awareness.

Behavioral Economics

The awareness of constituents and leaders then influence performance, especially in completing task beneficial to religious beliefs on economic discoveries. The literature illustrates traits exhibited despite the inherent dangers or ill-advised effect it may have on one's future outcome. Spiritual matters may confound actions or clarify behaviors exhibited because of religious teachings. (Peifer, 2008) Lending institutions are doing their best to accommodate members of faith-based organizations. (Harris, 2001)

A religious foundation in economic matters increases the likelihood that faith-based organizations can acquire expert knowledge to provide for its members. Investing institutions have initiative that lean beyond a social aspect to one with moral underpinnings (Baruch, 1999). People develop habitual behaviors regarding financial expenditures resulting in an almost predictable outcome. (Dent, 1998) The development of new behaviors and an explicit resolve to create an existence free of financial burdens is a noble objective. (Wolgermuth, 2008)

One of the ultimate objectives the literature seems to illustrate is a desire to create organizations that adhere to social, environmental, and economic concerns collectively. Seeking only the bottom-line profits of the organization no longer makes corporate sense. (Beynon & Maad, 2010) Behaviors that are conductive to innovative initiatives to bring constituents together are more valuable than individual interest. Consumer behaviorism and cognitive characterizations represents the need to understand the minds and actions of economic success. (Koonce, 1993)

Emotional accounting is an unrecognized factor in the reason's constituents create reasons for expenditures. Whether an individual is spiritual or not, the desire to acquire goods and services even in the light of uncertain circumstances is important. Federal regulatory elements have arisen to reduce the probability of another financial crisis. (Office, 2006)

Conclusion

The exhaustive literary search captured the relevant study's available to fully explore the research effort. From the first findings on religion and money, to the recent discoveries on how biblical economic determines one's beliefs. The crux of the research was to determine if external factors, one's beliefs, or economic behaviors were the influencing factors of financial literacy for faith-based believers. The findings in this research filled a void in the inquiry on religion and money that laid dormant for a significant amount of time. This information is critical to faith-based organizations that have faced an excruciating reality during the financial crisis of 2009.

In this qualitative study, the finding could be subject to other interpretations, meanings, or alternate realities. The findings suggestion several methods geared towards financial increases, such as avoiding negative behaviors, participating in religious events, or following designed specifications to achieve intended results. The limitations offered by multiple suggestions serve as gander for future research, which is discussed in another section of this dissertation.

The primary actions and inactions were the necessary behaviors that needed to be identified and provide a vital link to either avoiding sin or involvement as the precursor to financial literacy. The work has connected the germinal study and its most current findings together adding to the body of previously published literature. It resulted in a fully developed economic message that can be employed as an individual and organizational practice.

DR BLAKE'OLOGY

Bro/Dude/Hustler/Hold on there fella! What are you talking about?

Relax, relax, I had to draw the plan out and let them know where I was going with the information. You cannot just roll up to someone's Church and say, "Let me talk to your peep's about money?"

Richard, Johnnie, and James, the Head Usher would have happily laid hands on me and escorted me out the front door.

The idea here was to find out what folks knew, what has been done about it, and then put it in a picture. Seeing, is believing for some and to know where your people are can help you guide them.

Summary

Boulding (1952) asserts that individuals intending to avoid 'sin' have a propensity to develop behaviors consistent with wealth creations.

The Lehrer (2008) argument connects behavior as the centerpiece of individuals gaining access to economic success because of religiosity. Either systematic religious involvement or an aversive behavioral trait to avoid 'sin' is the catalyst for constituents to make habitual financial changes. Estelami (2009) further asserts cognitive behavior is at the root of creating an altered monetary outlook for conscientious constituents who want to make effective financial decisions. Financial information and education play a role in learning, but it is the active behaviors of the individual, that is most important when making the best financial choices.

The literature review identifies, described, and explained fundamental concepts vital to sustain the research effort. Principles necessary to illustrate behavioral economics of faith-based constituents create a platform to solidify pertinent findings. The exhaust of the review results to identify and set up the ability to answer the research question emphatically. As the impending influence of financial literacy combines inspiration with faith-based constituents, the right resolve is sure to follow.

The impending changes in the financial stability of our culture in the next 10 to 15 years will result from congressional budget office and the government's resolve for economic change. (Gramp, Willie, Pickford, Hoople, & Kiska, 2010) Mental accounting and hyperbolic discounting are an intricate part of the overall demeanor of financial literacy even in the realm of faith-based constituents. Principles of transaction utility and acquisition utility, influence the core beliefs established by the mental accounting traits in this research. Hyperbolic discounting concepts are at odds with religious constructs, thus adding to the conflict of financial influence. Future generations can undoubtedly glean from the implications to leaders and financial professionals who have the fiduciary responsibility to educate the average consumer. Faith-based constituents are in turn at the heart of initiatives to proliferate the prosperity of a peculiar group of people. (1 Peter 2:9, KJV)

.3.

METHOD TO THE DISCOVERY

A DISCONNECTION exists between faith-based epistemology and the influence of financial literacy based on economic behaviors. (Harris, 2001) The faith-based community's teleological (God's will) monetary advantage collapsed along with the ongoing financial crisis. (Neuman, 2003, p. 158) Religious doctrine and teachings about being in debt or being a borrower has not prevailed any greater than those of non-faith during the economic recession as 90% of congregational members are in some form of financial debt. (Harris, 2001).

DR BLAKE'OLOGY

The interviews were the bomb! I was surprised yet convinced that I was on the right track. There was this sneaky suspension that people were talking a good game.

However, many were not taking the right steps to make things happen financially in life. Desires for money and wealth were high but getting to that point seems to slip through theirs hands.

So, how do I do it? How do I keep trying to? How do I stop half-stepping? How do I develop a path, a route, or a model, and follow it!

Talk is cheap! Look, if you are debt free, in the past five-years what investments, life program, or debt plan have you started? What does the next five-years look like? Stop waiting on somebody to bring you a hot stock tip, go find it yourself. Read a money book, attend a financial seminar, but be mindful before you take your steps.

How will you know when you have found a good buy, a great plan, or an awesome program? The spirit of the Lord will tell you. Some people call it your 'gut instincts', it's that feeling inside. That feeling that say's Man, that is it! This is what we have been waiting for 'Hustler,' let's jump on it!

According to Servon and Kaestner (2008), financial literacy refers to the ability of the individual to understand how to gain access to economic information and make use of financial concepts. The consequences for lacking the appropriate skill in financial matters can have an adverse effect on the future of a nonprofit corporation and the productivity of its members. (Drucker, 2008). Mainstream financial literacy collides with the faith realms monetary structural beliefs, as the ambiguity between the religious prosperity communication and influences of an uncertain economic horizon. Religious philosophical constructs impede common sense and conflicts with secular viewpoints that can adversely affect the future of the nonprofit corporation by reducing the ability of its constituents to tithe or live a quality lifestyle. (Harris, 2001)

According to the US Census Bureau, 78.4% of the people in the United States consider themselves to be of the Christian faith. This population statistic includes Protestant, Catholic, Mormon, Jehovah's Witness and Orthodox adherents to similar religious units. (US Census Bureau, 2011) The populace of the state of Arizona accounts for 9.7% of our nations inhabitants, and further expands the list to include groups such as Seventh-day Adventist, Assemblies of God, and Churches of Christ. (US Census Bureau, 2011) In Arizona, the Christian population is 1,946,000 adherents, and this number represents 37.9%, the largest group of adherents in the states self-described religious identification population. (US Census Bureau, 2011) This is a significant percent or ratio of Christian adherents in comparison to the total population in Arizona, and a favorable attribute to the case study. The case study tentatively identified church organizations with 2,000 or more supporters, each having a distinct ethnic composition. Believers for the case study included a sample from Baptist, non-denominational and inter-denominational supporters to provide good perspective for the research. The general sample group of 30 participants represents a relative level of adherents' relating to a size appropriate to the population for the case study.

The purpose of the qualitative case study was to describe the financial knowledge of a 30-constituent sample from local ministries in Phoenix, Arizona. Employing a direct experience design describes the comprehension of personal economics and to answer the question; does religious teachings on prosperity correlate into financial literacy to the degree its constituents can obtain and sustain wealth. (Estelami, 2009) The endeavor asked how information anchored in knowledge with belief translates into actions for personal situations to change financially in an adherent's life. In this chapter, the researcher described the research method and design appropriateness, data collection process, accurate validity, and meaningful data analysis necessary to identify the phenomenon confirmed to influence faith-based constituent's financial literacy.

Research Method and Design Suitability

Qualitative research is best when the examination seeks to inquire, describe, or explore a study challenge. Individual experiences are difficult to quantify but the ability to give a detailed account of the feelings, emotions, and other 'said' knowledge holds firmly in qualitative research. Court (2008) states that complex levels of truth and meaning are analytically described in qualitative research as ethical and personal challenges reckon. The true thoughts and intents of constituents are divided between the essences of societal acceptance and the acceptance of religious constructs for economic behaviors. Understanding what causes people to do what they do despite feelings, emotion or purely common sense beg to be differed. (Court, 2008)

Complex social phenomenon underscores theory as appropriate to the researcher who seeks to find the fundamentals to serve as a foundation. (Tucker, Powell, & Meyer, 1995) In qualitative research, during an interview, the relaxing environment encourages people to discuss issues that the researcher did not know about. This additional 'said' information could add immeasurably to the bottom-line of corporations determining why adherents make certain organization financial choices affecting performance, or how those choices guide household financial understandings. This rich data source could offer up perceptions, experiences, and genuine attitudes that build successful theory relating to altering organizational financial choices. (Tucker, Powell, & Meyer, 1995)

Conjecture based on sound fundamental research activities holds more substance as researchers develop concrete concepts that render solutions to increase corporate productivity. The objective is to garner solid inputs and, in turn, translated these inputs into explicit knowledge for users to implement into their daily financial lives. Another objective of the case study will be to create a rigorous research environment that renders a learning culture conducive to gaining knowledge from the research.

Five standards help identify the rigors of qualitative research: appropriate data collection and analysis, competent content, explicit subjectivity, balance, and cognitive assessment of values. (Tucker, Powell, & Meyer, 199) The collection of data leads the researcher's questions to answers without a stagnation of ideas or unimportant communicative dialogue. Next, intelligently collecting technical data for rendering an expert opinion is necessary for good research to be replicated in the future. Identifying theory based on the data comes from the intent of questions that desire a response to research propositions. Balancing these discoveries, with an accurate assessment of individual value systems in place, enables truth telling to occur throughout the research continuum. (Tucker, Powell, & Meyer, 1995)

Cochran (2008) states that instituting a distinctive strength enables an innovative knowledge with positive assumptions. The vivid nature of qualitative information helps to develop precepts yet unidentified, because of its reliance on multiple sources of data rather than a dedicated source. The variety of inputs allows a differing of perspectives to surface and yield results uncharacteristic of traditional discovery in a given research effort. This unorthodox method promotes change and ushers in a fresh way of viewing a long-standing challenge, such as financial literacy among faith-based constituents. (Cochran & Dolan, 1984)

Discovering the meaning of thoughts defines what the study intends to accomplish, while seeking associative interpretations of economic behaviors. Discovering how far perspective or inquiry can reach in deciphering the causality of economic conduct, resides in qualitative research, and for these reasons, this research method best suit explaining the research phenomenon. (Cochran & Dolan, 1984)

Direct experience case study research allows one the freedom to view a problem outside of the traditional analytical context, by providing more descriptive information to solve a pervasive social concern. Quantitative measures accurately depict the most prominent thoughts held by constituents, whereas qualitative measures illuminate empirical values of thought or intent of the individual. The benefit of describing the lived experiences of individuals who exposed their most intimate thoughts, provides a greater insight into the meaning of economic behaviors or influencers. (Waters, 2010)

The phenomenology design allows participants to illuminate on personal matters that can relate to purposes, or a common theme, along with the synthesis of responses from other participants. To capture the lived experience of participants, enable the salient factors influencing cognitive behaviors to surface that correlate to economic choices made by adherents. This explorative endeavor garners intuitive aspects of how participants implement 'said' knowledge and thus reduces or prevents researcher biases from influencing the results of sound financial decision illustrated by participants. (Groenewald,2004) The process allows the consciousness of constituents to release true feelings and emotions that trigger certain cognitive behaviors.

The experience of experiencing the consciousness of individual choices and the resultant behaviors, induce a realization of recurrent patterns in the lives of constituents. (Groenewald, 2004) Visiting each Church in the study, listing to what was taught in the Sunday Service, attending ancillary classes held by the organizations, provided rich insight into their cultures. Profoundly capturing the images and words expressed by contributors provide powerful insight into what is influencing the economic behaviors of constituents. Understanding the interactions between emotions, feelings, and actions expressed in the form of behaviors, create an essential learning process. (Gallagher, Rocco, & Landorf, 2007)

Faith-based constituents' unique resolve, encompassed a desire to please a higher power, and experience an inner peace that encourages creativity. (Gallagher, Rocco, & Landorf, 2007) As the ultimate source of provision and purpose, spirituality ushers in a sense of meaning and purpose adherents aspire to achieve. (Gallagher, Rocco, & Landorf, 2007) The direct experience approach opens the door, and provides access to matters dear to the hearts of those who cleave to their faith. This again, illustrates the reverent feelings and emotions holding constituents, open to interpretation by this research effort.

The design gives participants freedom to respond to questions without the fear of reprisal, reprimand, or reluctance to authoritative discourse. No right or wrong answers exist when seeking answers; only those issues an individual is dealing with currently in life. Rossiter (2008) states that qualitative research depends emphatically on the skill of the analyst, and this too was a basis for an optimum research choice. Financial literacy is at the heart of this research, and understanding the cause or reason for faith-based constituents failing financially, is a troubling matter for the nonprofit industry.

Studying religion requires 'said' insights, and analysis aspects of faith, and it would be best to use a design akin to the same vibrant thought pattern. Gallaher (2007) describes phenomenology as a reflective process in which the researcher must seek internal emotions, energy, and lived experiences as a guidepost to understanding. This process relates spirituality as a learning theory, as it potentially enhances creativity in constituents to become fluid in their viewpoint. According to Creswell (2007), the meaning of multiple constituents lived experiences leads the researcher to the essence of an experience. (p. 57)

An approach that concentrates on consciousness, while exploring the core of "lived" experiences, and reflections of cumulative occurrences that result in unsaid meanings. Choosing a case study is optimum for the research as it transforms explicit knowledge into a new 'said' behavior beneficial to the constituents. (Gallagher, Rocco, & Landorf, 2007) The ultimate resolve would be to identify patterns of being, and channel those behaviors into productive resolves to influence economic behaviors conducive to financial literacy. In doing so, a direct experience research process would restrict or prevent personal biases from infiltrating the research efforts, and provide solid reflections of constituents input. (Groenewald, 2004)

Research Questions

The study described how, and if, participants are aware of their economic behaviors, and if they can or are able to make change in their situation.

1. What are the sentiments that influence financial literacy and its effects on recreating economic success after learning about monetary principles?

2. How does one transfer teachings on religious prosperity to the knowledge of choosing financial products and services by a group who is unknowingly self-constricted by religious impediments?

3. Do faith-based constituents who discern religious doctrine of wealth know fundamental principles of financial literacy?

4. How important is it that faith-based constituents who discern religious doctrine of wealth know fundamental principles of financial literacy?

5. Do faith-based believers who understand religious doctrine about building wealth, exhibit behaviors that do not result in economic actions that relate to financial literacy?

6. How significant is it that faith-based constituents who discern religious doctrine of wealth know and exhibit religiosity resulting in economic behaviors that relate to financial literacy?

Population

The study's sample consisted of 30 faith-based participants that are official members at their local community church or place of worship. They are representatives from three different religious establishments in Phoenix, AZ. The sample was composed of a broad base of religious knowledge across the discipline of the faith Christian in different values. (Lehrer, 2004)

The intention of this case study was to describe and gather information from participants who share a common intrinsic worth relating to their personal economic belief systems. Although constituents 'have a common belief system,' the questions remain regarding what, or how, their belief system influences behavioral economics was a focus of the research effort. In doing so, their description of personal monetary values helped identify and develop any relevant spending patterns or themes. (Levav & McGraw, 2009)

Stricker Street Story

Financial Freedom, Debt Freedom, and or Financial Independence are all terms with intrinsic desires to help others do well. In some cases, this could include the purchase of a product, service, or program designed on an interdependence on artificial paradigms needing investigative support.

I began my journey as an Investment Advisor Representative for two reasons.

1. To help myself, and
2. To help my momma.

Going to other people was an afterthought, besides I felt others already knew this stuff. Everyone except me, my mom, and some us from around the way who had no clue. Then I had a flash back to my childhood again.

My mom would cook a big meal on Sunday's, a sizeable pot roast smothered in beef gravy and onions, some collard & kale greens cooked with hog maw, cornbread, mashed potatoes, sweet corn, a ham and a two-layered chocolate marbled cake. To top it off, we had a two-gallon bucket of Kool-Aid to wash it down with!

Then she would send me on a "Plate" delivery mission: across the street to Ms. Johnson, sometimes down the street to Mr. Pete, and then.... I said, "Hold up Momma". Now remember, it was just me, my momma, and sweetie in our home. I said, "Momma we can't be giving all this food away! We got to leave some of that food here for me"! Mom said, "Boy we got enough food here for you!" I ended up running two plates upstairs to ole man Gus and Mr. Marcels.

My mom was keen on taking care of other people, especially the elderly. In her heart, her mission was to ensure they had one hot plate to eat on Sunday's and during Holiday's.

My Life lesson - taking care of others to me, is helping God's people, and those who want the Lord's help. My heart's desire is to seek, find, and assist those who want financial change by Building Financial Literacy.

The selected religious organizations are purposeful samples of three prominent religious organizations in Arizona and can provide a good foundation to develop credible dialogue for future research. Data triangulation allows for the collection of data from multiple sources that either corroborate or repel the same fact or phenomenon. (Yin, 2009) The study of choice is the results of experiences obtain from encounters with parishioners who expressed a desire to achieve financial independence. Qualitative data enriches with 'said' knowledge and illuminates a resolve that can be implemented successfully and proficiently within an organizational structure.

The sample included three various denominations, 30 randomly selected adherents who attend religious services at three different establishments, comprising various ethnic groups, to collaborate and ensure significance across the general spectrum of religious doctrine taught around the state. According to Lehrer (2008), religiosity is a variable that defines the involvement of constituents in activities involving the main religious organization. The description of such activities allowed constituents to share how often they attend services or other parishioner activities. The involvement in such activities also allows the leadership in religious organizations to impart information that could be relevant to their members. However, constituents who lack religiosity or express meager inclusiveness in these events are not able to receive pertinent economic information. (Lehrer, 2004)

Christians from various establishments have differing concepts of measuring or attaining economic successes relevantly. Purposive or judgmental sampling of these specific religious groups of participants closely represents the prominent spiritual organizations within the chosen metropolitan area. (Neuman, 2003, p. 213) This type of sampling allows data to contrast, validate or yield new perspectives that could saturate or exhaust a subject matter into common themes. The intent of the in-depth investigation was to gain a deeper understanding to the types of cognitive or behavioral influencers exhibited by constituents selected for the interviews. (Neuman, 2003, p. 213) This approach was appropriate, as it allowed for input from similar belief systems surrounding a common ailment affecting the financial literacy of its constituents. To garner participants for the case study, the researcher intends to share the findings of the research once complete, to attract participants traditionally not prone to contribute to academic research. (Neuman, 2003, p. 14)

The data collection occurred in two methods, first is a face-to-face interview with each participant, asking him or her to discuss a series of question, and digitally recording the 45-minute conversation. This allowed specific types of probing questions to be asked, and the observation of nonverbal communications as the interview process was in progress. (Neuman, 2003) Capturing rich descriptions of the phenomena in their religious context is the focus, and the best means to accomplish this task. The objective is to ask question pertaining to constituent's economic experiences, feelings, beliefs, and convictions regarding personal monetary affairs. (Groenewald, 2004) In personal intimate settings participants feel the freedom to respond without having to choose whether a response is accurate or not, their purest thoughts flowed during the interview process.

Interviewing allowed personal interactions to drive the conversation, and this dialogue provided the richest content of information to be shared by individuals, and participants were more receptive to a smiling interviewer. During the interview process the researcher maintained meticulous records pertinent to each interview. According to Groenewald (2004), the nonjudgmental evaluations encompass four types of field researcher notes significant to be obtained:

Observation Notes (ON) — *'what happened notes' are those items deemed important enough to the researcher to note and pertain to using a facet of ones five senses.*

Theoretical notes (TN) — *'attempts to derive meaning' pertaining to the researcher's thoughts, and reflections about experiences*

Methodological notes (MN) — *'reminders, instructions or critique' regarding the process while obtaining the information.*

Analytical memos (AM) — *is thorough end of the day summary or juncture evaluation.* (Groenewald, 2004)

Boulding's (1952) germinal exerts a focus on the complex process of economic development and the acquisition of an individual's capitalism to benefit the constituent's religious organization. According to his study, elements of a constituent's culture shaped by religious practices, were significant to the proliferation of the economic development. (Boulding, 1952) Understanding the practices or actions people take, allowed patterns of behaviors to evolve that have a specific outcome in relationship to financial dexterity. Boulding (1952) teachings of religious leaders and their influence on the ethics and the development of intellectual capital within the individual are significant indicators. The study identified importance of religious ideals, practices, and institutional involvement as significant contributors to societal power or organizational survival. (Boulding, 1952)

Boulding's (1952) study included religious groups who were Jews, Conservative Catholics, and Moderate Protestants. In his study, Jewish constituents promote gaining intellectual capital, as Moderate Protestants focused more on family values, thus each were at the opposite end of the spectrum when gaining intellectual capital. Catholics and Moderate Protestants are in the middle of discoveries, having gained neither intellectual nor the development of the family as predominant character trait. (Boulding, 1952)

Lehrer (2008) researched the role of religion and its influences on the behavior of constituents, and its effect on economics, as well as demographic factors. The Lehrer (2008) also survey participants to gain insight into their involvement in religious affairs in relation to economic development. According to Lehrer (2008), a constituent involvement in religious activities is consistent with positive influences upon their employability in the labor market, and on their ability to accumulate intellectual capital. The results of Lehrer's (2008) study shows the influence of frequent attendance and involvement in religious activities as a determining success factor, with less emphasis focus on individual achievement.

One common technique employed by the research effort was the administration of a survey tools to measure levels on understanding. (Castaneda, 2004) Boulding (1952) and Lehrer (2008) each surveyed participants to garner the valuable information pertaining to economic influences and religion. Survey information primarily allows for measurement of the retention of information by attendees, more so than describing influencers of economic experiences in a constituent's life. Prior research focuses on the external character traits, a constituent's ability to apply knowledge, or a reflection upon influences from religious involvement in organizational activity. These are pertinent measures to the developmental process of one achieving economic success in life that need an astuteness of 'said' knowledge to comprehend the financial resolve for monetary realization.

Each participant completed an informed consent authorization before the research effort began, and received a debriefing afterwards. (Neuman, 2003, p. 513) The information is confidential and maintained in encryption files that have password protection and was discarded after three years. The informed consent form outlaid who the researcher was, the context of the dissertation subject matter, and an assessment of the individual's role within the research. The informed consent was obtained and stored in a secured digital electronic format and transferred encrypted into its storage location.

The NVIVO 9-software suite for qualitative research was the chosen electronic filing platform to maintain and safeguard pertinent research documentation. Participant influence is taken into consideration when creating the consent procedures, as oftentimes, subjects could be inadvertently influenced by the professionalism of the researcher. (Neuman, 2003, p. 513)

The privacy of constituents' information was always secured and kept, and the information for each interview session has a code to safeguard the identity of each participant. Also, after each interview session the researcher ensured the participants of the safe-keeping of the responses they have just given. (Creswell, 2005, p. 218) The researcher offered a copy of the summary from the results of the survey to participants for their own personal gratification. The subjects who participate in the study provide detailed descriptions of their feelings associated with financial matters. This is a sensitive area for many individuals, just as equally important as the subject of religious beliefs. Combining two of the most sensitive topics in one research effort is understandably a sensitive issue, therefore access to any information was limited. (Cooper & Schindler, 2003, p. 123)

The confidential identity of the geographic location of the research site remained unidentified to ensure anonymous indications. The three ministry's location in the Phoenix Metropolitan area of choice is a selective process with access given by its local leader. The initial contact with any potential subject was with the permission of the proper authorities of the chosen ministry location. Once the location and access to the participants occured, the researcher provided a detail description of the congregations, any denominations, and their total membership size. The potential target locations conducive to the study consisted of organizations with a sizable membership group of 500 constituents or more thus, providing the researcher with the probability of selecting quality subject from a larger audience of participants. (Cooper & Schindler, 2003, p. 80)

A diverse representation in the proposed case study includes a mixture of various ethnic nonprofit organizations from the religious establishments, to ensure a complete research assessment on faith and finance discoveries. (Creswell, 2005, p. 531) The case study includes Christians with triangulation between the different nonprofit organizational group members to round out the case study. Triangulation of the data, confirms construct validity, as multiple sources or participants providing several measures of the same phenomenon. (Yin, 2009) The racial and ethnic composition of each faith is different, and the social classes have various similarities only differing in theological processes. No study exists in this geographic location about faith-based financial literacy, and the topic proposes could have fundamentally differing significance across belief systems. (Neuman, 2003, p. 528)

The descriptive data collection through a series of interviews and observations mixed behavioral economic theory and decision-making with faith-based ideology. (Estelami, 2009) Focusing on 'said' knowledge expressed by the cognitive behaviors and knowledge founded upon personal experiences revealing the causal nature of monetary attitudes. The research effort required descriptive accounts of participant's economic behavioral life occurring over different cultures with similar religious affiliations. The research questions guided the data collection process in two distinct fashions first; the process was seeking the level of financial knowledge a participant possessed. Second, to what degree were participants acting upon the information, that lead to the execution of having tangible results, to confirm the understanding of economic principles. (Neuman, 2003, p. 39)

The data collection process of interviews provided more salient information to answer the research question and provide compelling responses for the entire study (Neuman, 2003, p. 95). During the collection process the interviewee was asked specific questions along two continuums of thought. Logical significance and progression, describing the level of importance of a financial matter and what the participant was doing to acquire or resolve the economic issue. Respondents were free to speak and answer questions until they felt as if they had clearly provided an adequate answer to what the questions meant to him or her. The interviewer conducted and recorded the process while research notes were taken and shortly thereafter transferred into the NVIVO Software. Participant attitude, observation measures, and performance measures were significant indicators for annotation. The adherents must complete the same standard procedures for their goals to complete the interview is met. (Creswell, 2005)

The data collection during and after an interview allowed the participant to feel at ease knowing there was no right or wrong answer to the responses. The case study obtained a descriptive understanding of economic experiences influencing constituents who base monetary principles upon religious foundations. In general, the research was to drive the researcher's efforts to join-in with the participant while giving them the opportunity to receive cognitive assistance. A personal experience was the core influencers to the individuals' belief, and forms the rationale for one's perceptions and behaviors. The case study did not intend to gauge the level of financial knowledge a participant possess, but to describe what actions were taken towards financial solvency. Qualitative research of this kind seeks an interpretation or critical thinking in the social sciences in describing religious economic affiliations. (Creswell, 2005 p. 139)

The primary instruments for the data collection were verbal responses to questions drawn by an open-ended questionnaire that solicited a response. The verbal responses were merely a tool to guide the conversation in a direction that the participant felt comfortable enough to engage in a conversation within an environment that was conducive to sharing. A simple approach to a complex issue sets the environment at ease, and enables the conversation to continue and finish in its entirety. The distinction is that the interview is a short-term, secondary social interaction between a researcher and the subject. (Creswell, 2005, p. 295)

The secondary instrument for the data collection, was interview-questions driven by a Likert-type scale response, the intent of which was to use dialoging with 'said' knowledge of adherents externalized into explicit knowledge in the form of actionable knowledge. (Argyris, 1996; Nonaka & Nishiguchi, 2001) The rating had four-quadrant category that depended on the importance and performance of the responses to the financial literacy interview. The Likert-type scale (see Figure 1) initiated the discussion of financial literacy and provided the insight into the progressive actions of adherents and their economic behaviors, based upon what was important for them to act upon. Adherents completed a coded survey, and then they discuss the merits and contents of the survey, and what influences cause them to exhibit or pursue certain economic endeavors.

The Financial Literacy Likert-type survey questions identified areas of interest that a family or individuals feel were important enough for them to acquire the knowledge in that economic subject. A five-point scale measured the level of knowledge, as the participants feel comfortable with responding. The Likert-type scale identified the causal relationship between named attributes, extractions from observing the complexity of the gap in financial literacy. (Argyris, 1996)

The Logical Significance scale related to the adherents perceived level of understanding in that subject matter of monetary importance. The Logical Progression scale indicated actions taken toward achieving a financial goal at a specified level. The logical significance (importance) correlates to the logical progression (actions taken) questions to provide a picture of personal performance. For instance, Logical Significance question #1 asks how well participants know investments. Logical Progression question #1 identifies what actions, behaviors, or if any progress made towards the principle of investing in the financial arena. A graph plotted the progress and grouped the results into four categories, Low Importance/Low Performance, High Importance/

Low Performance, Low Importance/High Performance, and High Importance/High Performance. (Argyris, 1996)

This survey was an objective tool to discover what the participant knew, what they are actively doing in an identified area, and not what the adherents perceive the researcher, or the case study wanted to hear. The results were plotting along an X and Y-axis, placing participants into the categories of Financial Literacy. In doing so, the study received salient points as described by those closest to the issues who was the participant, the one who was experiencing the proposed gap in financial literacy. The questions were not specific but designed to allow the participant the freedom to describe their interest, attitudes, and values of the subject. The survey aimed to appeal to one's knowledge, appeal to actions that measure the distinction, and add a tangible degree to fill the gap in financial literacy. The case study described or explained the phenomenon not necessarily measuring the financial knowledge of the participant.

Figure 1. Likert-type scale
1 = Not at all, 2 = a slight extent, 3 = a moderate extent, 4 = great extent, 5 = mastery level

Financial Literacy

Logical Significance	Important
1. How well do you know investment?	1 2 3 4 5
2. How important is life insurance?	1 2 3 4 5
3. Rate your knowledge of fixed/variable interest?	1 2 3 4 5
4. Give the importance of a retirement plan?	1 2 3 4 5
5. How important is your credit score?	1 2 3 4 5

Logical Progression	Performance
1. Do you read your investment statements?	1 2 3 4 5
2. Did you read your personal insurance policy?	1 2 3 4 5
3. Read the fine print on credit card statements?	1 2 3 4 5
4. Do you fully fund your IRA?	1 2 3 4 5
5. Do you use a written financial plan & coach?	1 2 3 4 5

The second instrument chosen to capture the essence of the phenomena was an interview that allowed the researcher the means to apprehend an awareness of the situation at hand, by inviting candid responses to the case study questions. A one-on-one interview provided a private setting that allowed participants to feel at ease and free to comment without fear of reprisal or disapproval. The interview was an information-seeking tool that elicited information from respondents or informants. (Schwandt, 2007, p. 92)

The process was suitable to the researchers chosen profession and allowed for a smoother transition between the role of the research professional and participant. (Cooper & Schindler, 2003, p. 73)

The questioning was investigative and caused constituents to reflect upon the foundations of the knowledge they possess, and what they have accomplished thus far financially. The intent of the interview was to inspire an engaging conversation, opening dialogue that revealed the true feelings and emotions fueling actions that result in economic choices. Combining the proposed Likert-type scale with the detailed research from the in-depth interview was a means to concentrate on the phenomenon. (Schwandt, 2007)

The NVIVO 9 software was the primary and viable tool that interpreted recordings, surveys, and the instrument validation had proven to be a reliable tool in the academic community. The unit of measurement for collecting the data was personally interviewing 30 faith-based constituents of various ethnic, social, and geographical locations in Arizona. Conducting the research required 45-minute sessions conducted with at least 30 minutes of reflection time in-between interviews. The goal was to conduct five pre-scheduled interviews per day over a two-month period to accumulate the data necessary for completing the case study research.

As an incentive for completion of the interview the researcher proposes the issuance of a copy of the research paper as a reward. This information was offered after the participant completed the interview and to respecte those whose only intent was to help in the research program. The researcher used telephone calls and e-mail to set-up the appointments and confirmations to reduce cost. (Cooper & Schindler, 2003, p. 328)

According to Cooper and Schindler (2003), reliability dealt with the accuracy and precision of the measuring procedures. (p. 226) Reliability in the case study was demonstrated in triangulation, using the three different organizational faith groups to provide confirmatory data on the same phenomenon. The response from various Christian constituents' descriptive illustrations of their economic behaviors and epistemology's, and triangulation developed the research questions. The researcher ensured the results were reliable because the phenomena existed in three different organizational occurrences. (Cooper & Schindler, 2003, p. 226)

A measure is valid when it yields a description or estimate of a phenomenon consistent, different, accurate, or real. Three major ways to confirm the validity of the completed case study:

1. Content Validity – the interview questions confirmed two truths about the phenomenon, logical significance, and progress. First, it described how much constituents knew about their faith and financial astuteness. Second, it described what actions, if any had been taken to implement the knowledge.

2. Criterion-Related Validity – this measure relates the study as it identifies exactly what knowledge and actions need to fully comply with the research effort. The criterion had no right or wrong answer.

3. Construct Validity – the measurement obtained was relevant to the theoretical concepts as it identified gaps in financial literacy influenced by religious teachings.

Data Analysis

Analyzing the data composed of different subject areas separated into two categories triangulated between the various adherents, financial literacy, and the emergence of the phenomenon. The researcher sought the similarities and inferred meaning between the descriptive data in understanding the explicit and implicit knowledge basis, and the adequacy in answering the responses by the subjects. As the inferred patterns of similarities formed and emerged across cases, it illustrated the depth of the phenomena. (Neuman, 2003, p. 444) The chart below depicts the initial thinking process of the analysis and where the gap in financial literacy existed.

Figure 2. The Direct Experience Gap
Source: Modified from Gallagher (2007), p. 475

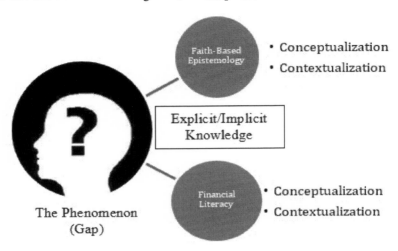

Making sense of the responses to the data allowed themes of economic significance to emerge and either naturally connected or disconnected with other participants. For instance, as a participant answers question one in the logical significance portion of the interview tool, the response translates into actions the subjects had taken. (Appendix A)

When a subject describes investments or investing in the market an action was done in the logical progression. The responses began to take form as the descriptions from participants from differing faiths illustrated the answers to the same questions. The intent was to convert the elements discussed and their meaning into an abstract form of a concept. Each concept depicted the significance and progression of economic importance in the study inferring to the phenomenon, a gap between financial literacy and faith-based epistemology.

A six-step process to analyze the data included data collection, preparation for analysis, reading data, coding of the data, identifying descriptions, and themes. (Neuman, 2003, p. 231) This was a simultaneous inductive and deductive process by taking the detailed transcriptions and notes of the ensuing generalities represented. (Cooper

& Schindler, 2003, p. 231) In the Appendix A, the main subject areas cover personal asset accumulation, protection, and religious inference relevant to the individual. In the researcher's experiences, these subject areas present the most challenge of economic understanding to individuals and represent basic understandings.

This data analysis method is the choice because it was the best way to understand the essence of the phenomenon from the individual's perspective. Economic research efforts were quantitative in form and resulted from numerical data based upon what was explicitly known about a subject. Approaching the research effort from a qualitative study by describing a phenomenon allowed for a rich descriptive technique. Accounting for what the individual believes was relevant to the understanding of economic factors derived from faith-based epistemology.

Participant Status

The participants were adult learners who were employed on a full-time basis and were randomly chosen or volunteered for the discussion involving financial matters. The typical participant was married, ages 25-45, and had 2 children and their income earnings were above the poverty level of $21,954. (US Census Bureau, 2011)

Participants within this demographic model assumedly would have the propensity or desire to obtain financial literacy. The acquisition of such information or knowledge could prove immeasurable to an individual's economic future. This method of selection ensured that those who participate were able to do so with no intent on personal gain. This made certain the integrity of the research effort and provided rich data during the interviewing sessions. To improve the financial literacy of mature constituents was an intriguing challenge, adults typically do not attend school, as do younger workers and tend to not have an interest in generic financial literacy classes. (Servon & Kaestner, 2008)

Behavioral Traits

The traits observed included exploring how financial literacy was important in four basic facets of being a well-informed, well-educated consumer. Consumers can make improved decisions for their families and improve personal economic security and well-being; give to vital and thriving communities by promoting community economic development. (Mimbs-Johnson & Lewis, 2009) The theoretical results from these traits provided the researcher with credible discoveries to assist in the faith-based leadership with a direction to guide its constituents. The best means to identify the traits was to allow individuals to control, to a degree, the amount and timing of information given during an interview session by the participants. (Neuman, 2003) The behavioral traits illustrated by each of the participants during the inquiry effort's, and the choices participants explained as the dialogue unfolds, was the basis of economic informational necessary to affect change.

During the research endeavors to identify the phenomena, there were other traits worthy of noting as the study progressed. The identification of the self-interest of people as the driving mechanisms to acquiring their desires, and when these desires are at an imbalance, trouble looms. According to Stucke (2010), an individual with a desire for self-interest seeks out while those who are unusually fair constituents are forced out or avoid conflict in an organization. The behavior people exhibit, has more to do with what they think is fair and equitable, than the desire to achieve financial independence may be a fair assumption. These instances, as in boycotting, where people would withhold their own gratification to address of express a certain collective concern. (Stucke, 2010) Obtaining financial solvency is the pursuit of a vast number of people groups, including faith-based constituents.

Financial literacy refers to the ability of the individual to gain access to economic information and make use of financial concepts. (Servon & Kaestner, 2008, p. 273) For this research gaining access to economic information was the access to financial tools, support from licensed financial professionals, technology or groups who provide information to its constituents. Professional financial recommendations can cost for personal services, but faith-based constituents seek the assistance from nonprofit entities for their free services. The assumption was that the economic resources one obtains from a professional for expert recommendations, could cost for personal services. The assumption was how could adherents make use of financial concepts if they cannot access the information. A participant is financially literate when their socioeconomic status enables them to acquire technological literacy to access financial information. (Servon & Kaestner, 2008, p. 280) This access empowers them with knowledge that when acted upon helped them employ financial concepts. (Servon & Kaestner, 2008, p. 281)

The results from the survey's and interviews connected the research questions with a resolve to create a viable financial literacy initiative for faith-based adherents. Adherents with an awareness can recreate economic success by learning monetary programs such as stocks, bonds, mutual funds, and real estate. Participants that exhibit religiosity, acquire the spiritual foundation, enabling them to employ 'said' knowledge to financial transactions (Lehrer, 2004). Responses to questions of allocating money's illustrate whether an economic principle is replicable and applicable in a setting. (Thaler, 1999) The questions pertaining to personal knowledge of financial terms such as Dow Jones, IRA, or 401K illustrates an awareness of knowing fundamental principles of financial literacy. Adherents who can discern religious doctrine have the tendency to read their religious text, also read their financial documents. (Lehrer, 2004)

Summary

This chapter described the research method and design appropriateness, data collection process, accurate validity, and meaningful data analysis necessary to identify the phenomenon influencing faith-based constituent's financial literacy. The implicit and explicit knowledge gained during the interview process was expected and did shed a meaningful light on the findings. In the following chapter, the expectation was to find the common casual nature or theme depicted in the interviews that created an opportunity for actionable learning. (Argyris, 1996) The researcher anticipates capturing the essence of this phenomenon to be recreated in an environment conducive to implementing an Actionable Financial Literacy Decision model. (AFLDM)

In Chapter 4, the objective was to determine how financially equipped faith-based constituents were, and to describe if this endeavor promoted the skill or confidence to make informed choices. To discover what actions constituents, to improve economic understanding in a faith-environment, and to ensure it, took what was conducive to building financial capabilities of acquiring the appropriate skill. (Holzmann, 2010) The anticipation of conducting the study heightens the awareness of the researcher in a fundamentally academic perspective.

. 4 .
THIS IS WHAT I FOUND OUT

The purpose of this chapter analysis was to report, in enough detail, the results of the qualitative direct experience case study. The objective was to build upon actionable knowledge, improve decision-making, and alter unprofitable behaviors of constituents. This chapter further indicated the causal economic behaviors of participants, from the interviews discussions that formulated potential ideas for an actionable learning model. The results from the Likert-type scale in the survey indicated a belief pattern existed among the participants regarding the relevance of financial matters, but the pattern lacked substantive actions or initiatives toward progress by the constituents. The NVIVO 9 qualitative software helped visualize the content of the one-on-one interviews with queries, tag clouds, and word-tree's results. Responses from the survey tool were converted into a Likert-type scale and visually supported a relationship to the descriptive data analysis of the NVIVO 9 interview results.

Survey Results
Seventeen male participants and 13 female participants took part in the research effort, from various ethnic backgrounds, contributing to a comprehensive strategy. The first and third location, where of a nondenominational faith, the second location was more of an inter-denominational faith. The survey participants were from several age groups: 20 – 30 (13.3%), 31 – 40 (23.3%), 41 – 50 (30%), and 51 an older (33.3%) of the participants. The ethnicities of participants were 30% African American, 16.6% Caucasian, 40% Hispanic/Latino, and 13% other. Several the constituents were married (56.6%), divorced constituents accounted for 16.6% of the participants, and 26.6% were single participants. Fifty percent of the participants earned $25,000-$35,000, 10%

earned $36,000-$45,000, 6.6% earned between $46,000-$50,000 and 33.3% earned $51,000 or more.

The scaling measures for each survey question used a weighted average that was calculation by dividing the sum of all the weighted ratings by the number of total responses to determine the mean score. The scores indicated participants deem 'Importance' as the greater measure with scores much higher on an aggregate basis than 'Progress.' The results meant that people knew what financial items were important, but lacked the discipline to do something about it. The importance of investments earned a slightly important rating of 2.5 whereas responses about the importance of life insurance earned a rating of 3.7. (see Figure 3) Understanding the difference between fixed and variable interest was moderately significant earning a score of 3.8, score and the significance of a retirement plan which earned a 4.0 that was the highest of all ratings (see Figure 3).

Figure 3 – Importance Likert Results

1 = Not at all, 2 = Slightly, 3 = Moderately, 4 = Greatly, 5 = Mastery level

Answer	1	2	3	4	5	Number of Response(s)	Rating Score*
How well do you know investments?						30	2.5
How important is life insurance?						30	3.7
Rate your knowledge of fixed/variable interest?						30	2.9
Give the importance of a retirement plan?						30	3.8
How important is your credit score?						30	4.0

*The Rating Score is the weighted average calculated by dividing the sum of all weighted ratings by the number of total responses.

Scores that related to taking action or performance were noticeably lower on an aggregate basis than scores of that denoted importance. The progress taken by constituents was notably lower than the importance of the corresponding vital topics. (see Figure 3) Participants slightly read their investment statement, resulting in a 2.4 rating, while reading insurance policies nudged a little higher at 2.8. (see Figure 4) The question that refers to "Reading the fine print on credit cards" had a modest measure with a slightly progressive mean score of 2.7 and funding an IRA/401K received a lower score of 2.3. (see Figure 4) The topic that received the worst rating for active engagement on both surveys, was the use of a written plan or financial coach. The rating for this category was 1.8 rating, closer to the rating of 'not at all'. (see Figure 4)

Figure 4 - Progression Likert Results

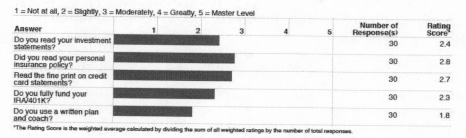

1 = Not at all, 2 = Slightly, 3 = Moderately, 4 = Greatly, 5 = Master Level

Answer	1	2	3	4	5	Number of Response(s)	Rating Score*
Do you read your investment statements?						30	2.4
Did you read your personal insurance policy?						30	2.8
Read the fine print on credit card statements?						30	2.7
Do you fully fund your IRA/401K?						30	2.3
Do you use a written plan and coach?						30	1.8

*The Rating Score is the weighted average calculated by dividing the sum of all weighted ratings by the number of total responses.

Likert-type Scale

Plotting of the Likert–type scale further solidified the findings from the survey tool, and illuminated what economic attributes participants felt were important, but lacked the necessary actions to do something about it. The five Likert-type scale results provided a striking visual of the content and how a person's beliefs can detach itself from the practices pertinent to economic development. (Barro & McCleary, 2003) The importance to financial literacy while executing economic performance takes a reduced role for participants, and the traits portray a stark pattern of behavior consistent across the plotting results of the five scales. (see Appendix D)

The plotting results of the, "How Well Do You know Investment" scale, illustrated that most participants did not compare the importance of investments, to the need to read investment statements. (see Appendix D) In the "How Important Is Life Insurance" plotting scale, a clear visual division emerged between the groupings of participants. (see Appendix D) Participants responses were inconsistent, showing that life insurance is important, but most participants do not read their insurance policy. The knowledge of fixed and variable interest received mixed reviews, as constituents had no clear understanding or definitive answer.

The existence of knowledge combined with a lack of actions was a prevalent pattern that evolved from the analysis. Most participants thought the subject matter of the survey questions were relevant to them as individuals, and to the case study. However, participants failed to realize how ineffective action and a lack of implementing financial programs had an adverse effect on an individual's future economic endeavors. The inaction was evident, as most respondents understood the importance of retirement planning, but considered the importance to be less significant than acquiring an actual retirement program. Lastly, participants indicated reading the fine print on credit cards statements, but it does not decrease the need to understand the lending practices of economic principles. Ninety-two percent of the participants rated the importance of having and knowing about a credit score according to the Likert-type scale as 'greatly' or 'masterly level' importance while a mere 1% had a plan and worked with a financial professional.

NVIVO 9 Results

The NVIVO 9 qualitative software was instrumental in providing a valid and reliable analysis of the responses to the survey instrument surfacing from the one-on-one interviews. NVIVO 9 gathered the data from extensive queries of 'word' frequencies, providing the 1,000 of the top words or phrases most frequently spoken during the interviews. The results appeared in a tag cloud (see Figure 5) in which the most frequently used words appeared in the largest and darkest letters.

Figure 5 – Tag Cloud

Then a text search was performed to refine the analysis based on the top words selected that showed during the referenced interview responses with a brief context relating to the words. The text search isolated the relevant subject matter pertinent or akin to participants' thoughts, feelings, and actions taken as a determinate to economic performance. (Lehrer, 2004)

The word frequencies were further refined and translated into a text search that identified a specific text, and expanded on the top two or three most frequent words. In defining words and further expanding on their usage, the process isolated the pertinent attributes influencing financial literacy and economic behaviors. (Huston, 2010) Responses to each research question identified a logical approach to what was important and what was happening in the economic lives of constituents. The data illustrated how the human cognitive systems were categorized into themes, or showed the limitations of an inability to cope with the complexity of financial stewardship. (Estelami, 2009)

The results of various word frequencies and text search queries continued to shed light on the pervasive thoughts held by the participants. A word frequency search for two of the most important words established the foundation for this study were the words 'God' and 'Budget' that revealed astonishing results. A frequency query for the word 'God' found that it permeated throughout the responses of this research endeavor in contrast to the word frequency search for 'budget' that did not reveal as many occurrences. The word 'budget' (see Figure 6) has a lower frequency rate than the word 'God'. (see Figure 7) The assumption is that an individual's religious belief in God has more influence on economic thinking than the importance of a budget. God has the upper hand when it comes to faith-based decision-making. (Barro & McCleary, 2003)

Figure 6 – Budget Word Tree

The infrequent use of the word budget implies that participants have a reduced resolve, or no use for a budget when it comes to having an economic discussion. (see Figure 3) The data further shows how participants describe their use of money, or how they would spend cash, rather than saving those resources for a specific item, process, or goal. The budget frequency visual considers that the use of a budget from a personal finance perspective is not as important in terms of its usefulness to the participants in the study. How participants use their funds is held loosely together by the need to provide for their family, and a desire to make a purchase during a typical financial transaction.

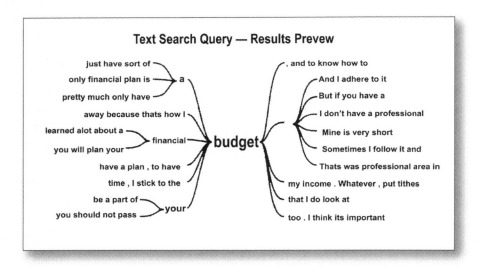

To view a comparative contrast of the Budget Word Tree versus the God Word Tree please follow this link.

https://lp.constantcontact.com/su/4nsVDS5/BooklaunchOct2019

The **God Word Tree** is too extensive to fit on one page of this book.

The use of God is pervasive throughout the entire interview process indicating the important role of religion and its belief's imparting influence on the consequences of financial decisions (Lehrer, 2004).

These graphic visuals provided a viewpoint to the words that were relevant to participants. The study provided a descriptive dialogue for each research question, and what influences enhanced participants' awareness of their economic behaviors toward making changes in their situation. The answers to the following research questions came from the answers provided to the survey responses, and the discussion during the one-one interviews. A combination of 52-word frequency, and text searches, were completed covering the 18 interview questions providing valuable insight as the top 1,000 words retrieve produced numerous texts spoken by the participants. The 52-word frequency and text searches created two or three major tag clouds and the top-three words were further refined with text searches, producing a word tree that enriched the context of those conversations. Again, the word frequency and text search query were instrumental in providing clarity to the complex a qualitative analysis of words spoken during an Interview.

The following descriptions and short quotes show how financially equipped faith-based constituents are, and explore the desired skill or confidence necessary to employ informed choices. Discovering the importance and actions constituents engage in to improve economic understanding in a faith-environment, ensured it was conducive to building the financial capabilities of acquiring the appropriate economic skill. (Holzmann, 2010) The data collection process was enlightened, as the study reinforced the awareness of a need for an actionable financial knowledge perspective necessary to increase financial literacy.

Research Question Answers

The answers to the research questions explained the insights gained from the survey tool, Likert-type scales, and NVIVO 9 analysis conveying the viewpoints of the participant. The results from the survey tool added to the findings descriptions by providing numerical meaning to 'said' behaviors. The number of total responses was divided by the sum of all weighted ratings that provided a mean score. This average formed the basis for measurement in the Likert-type scale by describing and explaining the answers to the research questions in a number. One of the purposes of the research was to find answers to the research questions and the responses were as followed:

1. What are the attitudes that influence financial literacy and its effects on recreating economic success after learning about monetary principles?

    a. What do you know about investments, or investing in the market?

The purpose of this question was to discover a participants' understanding of what, or how, a stock purchase is made to accumulate wealth, and then determine their understanding of bonds and how these purchases provide the security of a fixed return. To define their understanding of mutual funds as a collection of stocks mutually owned by a collective group, and the important aspects of real estate as a fixed asset purchased with the intent to increase in value. The participants spoke of how they were not '...too much' knowledgeable of investments. The participants in the survey answered, 'it is important' on average (2.5, slightly), but do not know much about it. In fact, respondents on an average (2.4 slightly) read their investment statements. These despairing results in respect to the awareness of the market created a situation in which deceptive or uneconomic decision-making can loom. (Estelami, 2009)

    b. What do you know about, and how important is life insurance?

References to the importance of life insurance included views of being especially important, very important, and extremely important. Constituents felt insurance was beneficial for the well-being of the family but lack the academic skills or personal desire to read a life-insurance policy.

    c. What is a credit score? How important is it?

In response to what was a credit score, participants described the effect or influence of a score but did not identify the components of a credit score. Constituents' descriptions included how rating agencies attached a number or score to an individual to measure a persons' worthiness to borrow money from a lender. No participant could identify the various components that make a credit score such as the cumulative amount of debt, the amount of new credit, payment history, or length of credit history. In fact, only two participant interviewee's had high credit scores, one had an 802 credit score the other had a 720-credit score, and each were women, who voluntarily shared their credit scores' without asking.

2. How does one transfer the teachings on religious prosperity into the knowledge of choosing financial products and services by a group who is unknowingly self-constricted by religious impediments?

   a. Which would you prefer $1,000 today or $10,000 in 10 years? Why?

The purpose of this question was to gain evidence or knowledge of mental accounting or hyperbolic discounting exhibited by group members. The finding was ambiguous with no clear preference for immediate cash, versus waiting later for a much higher payout. What made the question intriguing were the insights, reasoning, and remarks participants were glad to share. Constituents who preferred the $1,000 today shared these feelings, "Use it today," "take a vacation," and "an immediate source of income." Those chose to wait for the $10,000 in ten-years said, "Maybe worth more," "right now I don't need it," and "I'd be more mature." Surprisingly, the eldest participant and the youngest participant in the study expressed identical views of not wanting to wait ten-years because they, "Might not be here." Other participants' thought, "Wouldn't be worth," "seems like too long," or "I might be dead" as the uncertainty of a distant future dissuades them. The emphasis of placing more value on what an individual gain now versus the rewards of waiting for later is a continuously debatable subject.

   b. What do you know about the Dow Jones? What does the Dow Jones do?

Attendance at religious events had no bearing on learning the purpose and meaning of the Dow Jones Industrial Average. (DJIA) The typical response reflected attitudes such as, "I don't know much," "I am really not familiar," and "I hear it on TV." There are 29 economic indexes reporting the monetary movement throughout the world and they include nine indexes in the U.S./America, eight indexes in European, seven indexes in Asia/Pacific, and five World indexes. (CNBC. Com) Two participants were close to correctly stating where the DJIA was reporting at the time of the study. Discussing the purpose of the other 28 indices with participants is inconsequential because the level of understanding requires additional instruction.

    c.   Where is the Dow Jones now? What are your individual financial strategies?

This question was troubling as constituents responded with a resounding, "Couldn't answer that question," "have no idea," and "I don't know where the Dow Jones is." These responses relate to the progress or action constituents have taken to understand market movement. Again, the DJIA one of 29 indicators used to monitor the economic movement of the world's economies and constituents are unaware of their significance.

In respect to financial strategies the comments were, "I put money in certain bank accounts," "just stay the course," and "saving fifty-percent of my paycheck." These thoughts illustrate a worthy attempt to set aside resources or monies for future usage. Other constituents expressed, "Manage expenses," and "I have social security, I have an IRA, and I have an apartment house," clearly some participants enjoy solid financial strategies.

    3.   Do faith-based constituents who discern religious doctrine of wealth know fundamental principles of financial literacy?

    a.   How often do your read or study your religious text?

The response from this query was quite strong, as participants range from not as much to every day, six days per week or at least weekly. Disciplined study was also prevalent in the responses ranging from weekly, daily, or study sessions during the weekend. However, participants at the second research location preferred reading or studying spirituality documents or books not necessarily the Holy Bible itself. Constituents fully exhibited behaviors of practical biblical study habits but the content or topics of the study matter were not mentioned. As stated earlier, more than 2,350 scriptures relate to finances in the Bible and it is unclear if the topic of economics was one of the subjects during a given study session.

  b. Tell me what you know about fixed and variable interest?

Participants described fixed and variable interest within the context of a mortgage or lending situation from the standpoint of a debtor. Participants illustrated how a fixed interest rate is more desirable than the uncertainty of a variable interest rate. A small portion of the respondents understood that there is a fixed or variable interest rates that also exist as an investor. The collective response of the participants could be tainted by the recent housing debacle and the ongoing financial crisis the world continues to experience. Even so, biblical teachings suggest borrowing is subservient thinking to lending and that those with substance rule those who lack resources (Prov. 22:7). Despite being aware of this spiritual truth constituents cannot distinguish between fixed and variable interest as an economic growth axiom. The behaviors of faith-based constituents and consequently their mindset gravitate toward that of a borrower more than a one who accumulates wealth.

  c. How often do you read your investment statements? Stocks, bonds, mutual funds, or real estate, etc.?

The most prominent response to this question was, "I don't read them, in detail once" and "I don't think I have ever read them." The lack of reading an investment statement in detail only once or when the plan changed was not enough to keep one's pulse on the progress of an active investment program. This is clearly a lack of attention to investment detail exhibited towards an economic precept necessary to change behaviors. The insight confirms that either participant's do not know how to read an investment statement or are they merely not interested in doing so. Either way the lack of knowledge or the practice of reading an investment statement can lead to economic failure of epic proportions.

 4. How important is it that faith-based constituents who discern a religious doctrine of wealth know fundamental principles of financial literacy?

  a. Tell me about the terms of your personal insurance policy?

The constituents did not describe in detail the specifics of their personal programs with only two participants naming an actual life insurance company. The specific two comments, that referenced to an organization were, "Through Honeywell," and "through Minnesota Life," not necessarily household names in the personal insurance industry. The alarming responses by participants were, "Don't have a separate life," "I have never read," and "I don't have one." Theses references to not having insurance at all indicate a lack substance of translating doctrine to financial literacy.

      b.   What does the fine print on your credit card statement indicate?

The responses included that the interest rate was influenced by any late payments and could cause a rate change from single digit into a double-digit repayment rate. Constituents' expressed that the fine print shows the, "Company protecting themselves," "may vary," and that the interest rates are going to be "jacked up." The participants knew the potential cost and unfavorable outcome yet continued to exercise the use of credit cards. This is classic hyperbolic discounting as constituents ignore the long-term effects of credit usage to gratify immediate needs (Estelami, 2009).

      c.   What does it mean to fully fund a Tax Shelter? Example IRA or 401K?

The respondents stated that the IRA/401K is an important program to establish to secure one's future. The constituents reiterated "definitely important," "pretty important," and "extremely important" but actions taken to implement such programs are anemic. In fact, constituents responded to understanding of what it takes to fully fund a retirement programs as, "I am not sure," "I think," and "no payments are necessary." The clarity of what is essential to start a retirement program takes away from the probability of making an effective financial choice. (Huston, 2010).

     5.   Do faith-based believers who understand religious doctrine about building wealth, exhibit behaviors that do not result in economic actions that relate to financial literacy?

      a.   How often do you read or study your religious text?

The response to this question is significant as it indicates a suggestive basis for faith-based epistemology's influence on financial literacy. Participants said that they read or studying a bible, religious text, or spiritual books on a consistent basis. There were a few notable responses, "Once a week," "study my bible every day," and "a whole lot." This level of reading should culminate in at least a few specific responses to common questions about biblical prosperity teachings. The topic or title of what was being studied by participants were, "Basically study a title," "probably study information," or "study based on new thought." The subject of financial literacy or economic understanding was not mentioned specifically yet no other specific subject surfaced, either. Again, the study habit behaviors were obvious ranging from, once a week," to "six days per week," and "Friday – Saturday I study."

      b.   What are the spiritual scriptures that you adhere to regarding money?

The reply to this question was interesting as constituents' answers, "As far as trusting him," "Jesus gave us an example," and "Faith are my wages." These are the teleological remarks (God's way of doing things) constituents cling to concerning money. One respondent retort, "... Stuff is common sense" while another retorts "to be ride of money," has the understanding of money become a common occurrence?

      c.   What would you do with $100,000 after giving tithes and offerings?

The funds would be used. Participants stated a spending pattern, "I would probably go to Europe" or "I would purchase a property". On the other hand, a few ascertain a desire to, "I would probably want to invest some" and I would probably put another two — thousand in investments". The intent was to recognize the influence This question challenged constituents' ideal of budgeting, questioning their planning process for allocating a sudden windfall. This is when the concept of mental accounting surfaced in the answers as constituents merely described how of how a financial decision was made and defined by how unexpected financial resources received is treated differently by the person who receives the money (Estelami, 2009).

6. How significant is it that faith-based constituents who discern religious doctrine of wealth know and exhibit religiosity resulting in economic behaviors that relate to financial literacy?

    a. How important is attending Church Services?

Religiosity is an individual's active engagement or involvement in religious activities and how it affects economic outcomes for faith-based constituents. Respondents express the importance of attending church as, "Very important because it keeps you level," "very important to fellowship with others," and "I feel good." The intrinsic value gained from the involvement in religious programs, along with participation in a church activity provides constituents with a sense of togetherness. This accentuates the well-being and cognitive heath of the individual, ushering in chances of a better outcome in a decision-making process. (Lehrer, 2004)

The constituents describe the answers to this question by expressing the significance of attending church as 'very important'. The opinions expressed by constituents that Church is "a social outlet," "it feels good," and "it's a part of life." An intrinsic value such as lifestyle and consistent fellowshipping is a part of being Christian and promotes a healthy involvement in social activities. This behavior was a conduit for the exchange of spiritual growth and economic progression.

    b. How often do you attend, participate or visit your church?

The amount of time one spends in a religious setting in comparison to a commitment to economic success does differ. Most respondents said, "Once a week," some even "three-times per week," and the true road warrior, "four day's out of the week," to "easily five days a week". The extreme faith-based constituent said they spent, "Five to seven days a week" participating or visiting church. Constituents spent an average of 2.1 days per week participating in Church activities, which is hardly enough time to be considered an influencer or determining factor for monetary success.

The balance between spiritual involvement and the pursuit of economic endeavors needs to reach a spiritual and natural median. Efforts beyond a certain self-determined point begin to crowd any time set aside to take advantage of learning market activities. (Lehrer, 2008, p. 10)

   c. Do you have a financial professional? What written financial plans are you following and how often do you refer to its content?

The resultant behavior further confirms Estelami (2009) assertion that behaviors do not reflect a disciplined approach with a well thoughout plan or a decision-making process to manage funds. Constituents who regularly attend religious services express reluctance to seeing a financial professional. Remarks such as, "I don't have," "I don't use," or "...we are not following one" could stall one's economic success. Participants stipulate they, "No longer rely on a financial professional," "lost me money," and "paying the financial planner more than what they are making." The last few years of ethical and moral misdeeds by corporate executives and financial professionals have taken a toll on the confidence of the consumers as one participant retorts, "My written plan is, don't lose money."

While other participants express attributes of their current plan as, "Not following one right now," "mine is very short," and "I read periodicals." A small remnant share, "Commitment to work with a financial company," "a gentleman that works at Fidelity," and "my Dad is a really, really, good financial guy." Another participant shared, "I have a financial contact" with this approach constituents established a desire to partner with a professional, but not to rely solely upon a financial professional. Interviewee 17 shares some interesting insight: "Most of the people who are financial analyst or financial support people their main motivation is not sell you their time or their expertise. Their main motivation is to sell you something, this has been my experience. So, if you want an opinion on something very selective, it's very difficult to get an objective opinion". As the economy recovers and constituents gain confidence in an efficient economic system, consumers can once again seek to employ the skills of a financial professional.

Stricker Street Story

A strange (yet fun) ghetto game we played as kids, "Snatch Pops" and "50 – 50". So, if you saw your buddy coming out of the corner store with food, candy or a snack in hand you would yell, "50 – 50"! Which meant that the goods would have to be split between the two of you. However, if you were close enough to snatch the good out of your friends' hands and proclaim, "Snatch Pops & No 50-50"! this meant that the goods purchased now belongs to the claimant and the purchaser is out of luck. ☹

What one knows, versus the actions one takes, does not equal financial success.

My Life Lesson: *Sometimes it feels that way financially. When the paycheck comes in, Uncle Sam takes his first, a good chunk goes to taxes. Then a grip is taken by the bill collectors, mortgage/rent and the majestic car notes. When, or if anything is left over, then comes the time splurge. Wait a minute, what about the future?*

Summary

This case study provides salient content validated by insights into the thinking and cognitive behaviors relating to financial choices or resolve concerning monetary solvency. The contrast between what is important financially to participants, was surprisingly contrary to the behavioral traits exhibited to achieve the appropriate measure of economic success, helping to identify a criterion-related decision model. The Likert-like scales support construct validity as the results illustrated the weighted average of what constituents feel as significant to their fiscal lives versus any progress made to accomplish a monetary realization and clearly identified gaps in financial literacy. Participants have strong feelings for the importance of items relevant to the skill of their financial existence. (Huston, 2010, p. 296) The actionable measures taken to achieve economic success needs to encompass an ability to implement financial programs. (Houston, 2010, p. 296) Chapter 5 discovered models of effectiveness to employ to improve the faith-based constituents resolve to obtain financial literacy.

.5.

WHAT DO WE DO NEXT

THERE is a gap between faith-based epistemology and the influence of financial literacy based on cognitive behaviors. (Harris, 2001) The faith-based community's teleological (predetermined outcome) monetary advantage collapsed along with the ongoing financial crisis. (Neuman, 2003, p. 158) Religious doctrine has not prevailed any greater than those of non-faith during the economic recession, as many congregational members with 2,350 Bible verses discussing the topic of money, living in some form of bondage to debt. (Harris, 2001; Wolgermuth, 2008)

Church is a viable avenue for adherents to rely on when tough financial challenges infringe upon their existence; however, the Church is facing its own harsh economic reality. In fact, banks foreclosed on 200 religious' institutions in 2008 whereas only eight suffered this fate eight years earlier and virtually none a decade prior to that. (The Wall Street Journal, 2011)

DR BLAKE'OLOGY

The dinosaur found on this tour was the very distinct use of, "Budget" vs "God" in the financial case study. I was surprised yet expecting what was revealed.

God is the creator and finisher of our financial faith. The world we live in has systems created by those gifts by God (acknowledge or not) that we need to learn, understand, and to maximize.

Once again, Financial literacy is the ability of an individual to gain access to economic information and make use of financial concepts to make effective choices...

The gap between financial literacy's influences on faith-based epistemology exists within constituents' economic behavior, as it is not commensurate with obtaining and making use of financial information. A nonprofit organizational sustainability is dependent upon the dexterity, prosperity, and generosity of its constituents. Leadership's responsibility in guiding such organizations should address the key 'said' and explicit attributes to maintain corporate performance primarily through the profitability of its constituency. In the case of a nonprofit organization, a key indication of economic health is the encouragement and relationship between the internal and external stakeholders' economic success. The wealthier cohorts and constituents become, the more everyone can give, gain more wealth, and give again to the organization.

The fundamental theory guiding the recommendation is Actionable Knowledge infused with double-loop learning created by circumstances and environments conducive for economic education. (Argyris, 1996) Actionable financial knowledge employs intent consequential to the success of an individual's financial solvency compounded with the success of others. The external validity gains support from the causal responses of well-advised actions toward cognitive desires. Simply, this is achieved when constituents reach their personal goals, achieve fiscal success, and articulate actions as norms. (Lehrer, 2004)

However, a participant desire to achieve financial success appear to stall because of the ineffectiveness or a lack of their personal actions. Double-loop learning resolves the issue by instituting self-efficacy and bolstering constituents' learning with an innovative decision model exclusively monitoring and guiding monetary deeds. (Argyris, 1996)

Biblical references express a form of actionable knowledge about the spiritual wisdom of the Creator and the activities of individuals. One biblical scripture reads, "...The Lord is a God of knowledge, and by him actions are weighed." (1 Sam 2:3, KJV) In comparison, "...So, faith without works is dead..." this is another notable biblical scripture too (Jam 2:26, KJV). Actions and works, two important elements that require personal efforts to achieve change. The answer to filling the financial literacy gap defined in Chapter 4 was to design a specific model that was retrieval in the minds of constituents. The models design specification was directed toward intentional personal actions that produced the desired financial consequences. The idea relates to economic performances by acknowledging an omnipresence of knowledge and weighing the actions of individuals pursuing sustained growth. Personal choice made by individuals was the sign of achieving a level of accomplishment equating to actionable knowledge. The designs causality renders actions that fill the knowledge gap by consistently replenishing voids resulting from ineffective means to foster individual and organizational economic learning. This learning model exposes and helps correct errors in thinking that leads to actions and deeds creating a vibrant economic learning culture. (Argyris, 1996)

This is a viable decision model centering on an individual's intent to become financially solvent with sustainable economic behaviors. (Holzmann, 2010) The constituent must then retain the responsibility of exercising economic choices conducive to positive progress. This resolve is principally sustainable with religious or spiritual underpinnings leaning toward financial literacy. The five-point Actionable Financial Decision Model (AFLDM) contains two-spheres of influence, actionable behaviors and actionable knowledge. An Actionable Financial Behavioral Change model (AFBC) overlies the AFLDM exercising inquiry and exploration as a template for addressing each stage in the AFLDM with behavioral changes. The intent of AFLDM is to illustrate a way of thinking that one can share and teach to others not privy to financial counsel or education.

"A financially capable person is one who has the knowledge, skills and confidence to be aware of financial opportunities, to know where to go for help, to make informed choices, and to take action to improve one's financial well-being within an enabling environment for financial capability building to promote the acquisition of those skills." (Holzmann, 2010, p. 5)

As constituents progress through the five points of the AFLDM, efforts to detect and correct errors evolve from employing the AFBC model addressing constituent thinking. Patterns of thinking need to shift back to the consumer taking personal actions and not allowing constituents to exercise choices blindly or without ethical professional suggestions. Conditions of personal ineffectiveness combined with professional improprieties help home foreclosures spread like a contagious ailment, constituents especially need to alter this social trait. (Angelides, 2011)

Actionable Financial Behavior

The agent for managing economic behaviors is human intent in association with actions rendering performances relevant to financial success. The purpose of AFBC is to detect and correct errors in monetary thinking, leading to constituents in an organization thriving financially. The research findings confirmed that for agents of change to be effective, they must continual measure and evaluate five initiating yet distinctive fiscal activities. (Argyris, 1982; Argyris & Schon, 1996)

1. In what way do participants produce the economic actions intended?
2. How do the economic actions produce the intended financial effect?
3. In what way do constituents know that the economic answers that they are providing to the first two questions are not monetarily flawed?
4. How much confidence do constituents have in the economic answers provided in the first three questions above are not epistemologically/unrealistically distorted?
5. Can constituents maintain behaviors in relationship to these questions and then permit and inspire other individuals (or a larger collective) to recreate the same experiences?

Figure 7 – Actionable Behavioral Change (Argyris, 1996)

The purpose of the model is to foster economic behaviors directly relating to sustaining organizational productivity. The intended activities or resolve results in an increase in the corporate bottom-line and profitability. Epistemologically (unrealistic) distortions detect any interference with rationality, logical thinking, and faith-based influencers to decision-making defined by the first three stages. The idea is to allow those in positions of influence to become the support of confidence in the recreation of ideals for changing economic behaviors filling the knowledge gap.

The model is a "check and balances" for each of the five points in the AFLDM and ensures the integrity of the entire process. The model serves a recurrent measuring tool for actions, and their perceived or intended resolve to achieve organizational sustainability. As steps are taken to move forward the individual experiences growth and this improvement is necessary for the whole collective in a nonprofit organization. As the individuals get stronger, a nonprofit corporation's ability to provide for the consumer, satisfies internal, and external stakeholders. The resources gained have significance and the resolves assurance comes from a purposeful intent to alter corporate norms and suggestions toward individual profitability. (Collins, 2010)

Three Ideological Pillars

Another means of coupling financially literate stakeholder with a fiscal economically successful contributor is to be an Agent of Change. This element recognizes the 'Three Ideological Pillars' while implementing the AFLDM. What does it mean to "discern biblical doctrine of wealth"? Biblical doctrine (teaching) on wealth builds on devout (religious) premises and discusses three ideological pillars. Today, nonprofit organizations find themselves as a primary conduit or advocate for addressing financial literacy education for its constituents (Collins, 2010). The concept of the "Three Economic Pillars" fosters innovative thinking with relevant contextual meanings pertaining to faith-based instructions on wealth and the premises of measuring monetary achievement in which these pillars encompass:

1. Substance - possessing just enough to satisfy ones needs
   a. No Revolving Debt (minimal assets/cash)
2. Abundance – possessing more than enough to satisfy ones wants and needs.
   a. No Debt and substantial financial resources (Cash).

3. Rich's – satisfying wants, needs, and desires while using sub-
    stance and abundance to empower others.
    a. No Debt, substantial financial resources, and residual
        income.

The focus is not on the physical aspect of money that is subject to
change and is based on approval by the appropriate institution or societal viewpoints. However, the nominal amount of assets gained is
merely an indicator to measure and the level of wealth. The Three-pillar
is a checkpoint along the journey of financial solvency and constituents
can relate to its philosophical means. However, the intent is to create
and sustain the three ideological pillars to ensure the transfer of reverent (spiritual) principles as well as conventional actions for financial
literacy.

Actionable Financial Literacy

The Actionable Financial Literacy Decision Model (AFLDM) creates
a theory of economic omnipotence (EO), a learning viewpoint that rec-
reates economic learning in classrooms, boardrooms, and administrative offices. EO is a continual cycle of actionable learning, implementation, and evaluation perpetuating the connective behaviors in design
causality. Essentially when a constituent say's, "I don't know" the implied meaning is either the participant was not able to do so or they do
not know how to accomplish the task. As a guiding presence EO encompasses two spheres of influence and establishes five fundamental
revolving precepts to employ. The intent is for constituents to progress
cognitively from knowledge, to skills, to attitudes, and to new behavior that results in a definitive action leading process of EO. (Holzmann
2010; Kempson, 2008)

Figure 8 – EO and Actionable Financial Literacy Decision Model (AFLDM)

Actionable Financial Knowledge

contains the inputs (Information) necessary to apply and create the foundational intent of financial constructs that include ethical economic stewardship and money basics. The onset of double-loop learning creates circumstances and environments in which constituents learn financial concepts and lessons conducive to positive monetary productivity. (Argyris, 1996)

Stewardship

an individual's character trait indicative or rooted in religious affiliation refined by a learning or leadership model. A meta-analysis of religious education and knowledge translated into actionable measures that recreate learning experiences was necessary. Guidance based on the teleological influences was common and acceptable to members of the faith-based society. Implementing processes, teachings, and fostering behavioral modifications must be exhibited by the leader to foster change.

Money Basics

incorporates comprehending the value of money over time, the purchasing power of current and future dollars, and personal financial accounting models. The issue is that money a tool. People see money differently and it has changed forms and evolved over time. Money began as a bartering system, then the trading of animals, fabric (silk), coins, and paper; recently plastic (credit cards), now-cell phone applications like Square and PayPal. Understanding the transition of money and the altering state of money's existence keeps constituents attentive to the appropriate behaviors for creating wealth versus depleting resources.

Actionable Financial Behaviors

converts the inputs into outputs (Actions) in a usable form to apply the context of one's life to include investing, borrowing and protecting. The actions that one takes can infuse learning or it can deplete efforts rapidly to create and sustain wealth. A leaders self-maintenance concept includes, considering the efforts of cohorts, constituents, and pertinent stakeholders that cause growth. Exhibiting the proper leadership behavioral traits is crucial to the successful implementation of new economic behaviors throughout an organization.

Investing

encompasses saving money now for future expenditures through the practice of investing with vehicles such as stocks, bonds, or mutual funds. The idea of "putting some away" is a tactic espoused by participants in the study, as a means of describing the act of investing. Constituents in the study state, "A portion of some sort," 'certain things in certain pots,' and "money away somewhere." The clear indicator or resolve is to have an amount of money in a place when needed. Constituents can gauge what is put away by the 'three pillars" since there is not a specific amount reference in the study. A specific dollar amount would vary between individuals and corporations per se but the need to reserve some form of cash for the future needs to be accumulated.

Borrowing

brings future income into today using credit cards, consumer loans or mortgages all of which are debt instruments and should be balanced by the amount of one's assets. The effort to remain vigilant of ones thinking regarding be a lender/investor and not just that of a borrower is necessary for success in reversing a debt mentality. Constituents must embrace the nature of creating wealth by employing concepts that enable them to have money set-aside when needed.

Protecting
safeguards resources with the use of insurance or other risk management (mitigation) techniques. The transference of risk is a definition that applies to the concept of insurance and can be confusing. Constituents' need an understanding of the purpose of an insurance program is to protect assets, not necessarily to seek monetary gains.

The results of Chapter 4 provided a vibrant picture of the phenomenon of financial literacy in the faith-based community. Constituents desired an objective understanding of the economy and aspired to take advantage of precepts to improve themselves economically. Meager actions or reluctance while relying on fate, circumstances or the powers to be to reward them for being good was pervasive. Delving into Chapter 5, helped drive the answers and provide a template to inspire leaders to create, monitor, and implement financial actions. Constituents gained the awareness necessary to influence actionable financial knowledge that consummate in actionable financial behaviors that close the gap in financial literacy (Argyris, 1996).

Future Researcher
The crux of the Financial Crisis was the result of inordinate human nature confounded by inappropriate actions – individual inactions forged with a societal irresponsibility to account for human weakness. (Angelides, 2011) Through this in-depth analysis of personal responses to financial matters, several questions arose for possible future research. (Angelides, 2011) The nonuse of a financial professional was a notable subject that stood out in the results that could infer a reluctance to work with a financial expert. Some participants continue to work with financial professionals while the majority has abandoned the idea and retained control of their own economic destiny. It was conceivable that this behavior was becoming a widespread practice as the access to the Internet increased the admittance to economic information (Servon & Kaestner, 2008). One may ask, "How does this increased access to economic data equate to financial literacy?"

Stricker Street Story

One day we were playing speed pitch on the playground at School #35, Harlem Park Elementary School. (Long before it became a parking lot) The lot rule was if your hit the ball on the roof you had to go get it, so I did it and I had to get it. Now back then, there were other mischievous kids breaking into the door on the roof to damage the inside of the school. I knew better than that and I surely did not want to her my mom's screaming at me. Now, I was a at least a block away on a third roof.

Suddenly, I hear this load voice, "JOE, BRING YOUR BLACK *SS OVER HERE". It was my momma, with sweetie in tow, and I was in hot water. I received a world class lecture about being on the roof and to "think twice and calculate my actions" in the future. Momma told me, Ms. Myrtle, the neighborhood newscaster, sole watch party, and local snitcher on Joe told on me. (That was not the only time) It does take a village to raise a family. If it was not for the watchful eye of a concerned neighbor who knows what could have happened, so.

My Life Lesson: *Knowledge – Skill – New Behavior, I had received new knowledge from my mother about her reasons for avoiding scaling a 3-story building. Therefore, I had to invest in a secure risk /skill adjustment, requiring a behavior change. So, we purchased two extra rubber balls, a new behavior, now if a ball was hit on the roof it was a goner. We used a different ball to continuing having fun. Financially the goal is to gain knowledge, learn a new skill and create new behaviors relative to achieving success.*

Another key subject was the global influence of financial literacy and the guidance of first-generation immigrants living in the United States. New US citizens bring with them their customary financial ideologies from their homelands. For instance, one participant remarked, "...Life insurance isn't a product that is purchased or is not as important in the country I am from." These sentiments can permeate through several generations until an unfortunate incident, such as an untimely death forces constituent to rethink the logic and purpose of life insurance. How does immigration or international ideologies influence financial literacy for faith-based constituents in the United States and abroad?

Future researchers can further delve into the family structure to define the financial principles taught or untaught throughout the generations. They can explore how financial lessons are learned, or unlearned, and what principles if any are handed down to the next generation. What action is employed to ensure the proper financial step is recreated in the next generation and then the next? The precept of continual learning, evaluating, coupled with discovering financial errors are key to extending wealth creation throughout each generation. Exploring these questions from a qualitative standpoint emphasized the traits from a personal economic behavior standpoint while describing the phenomenology of financial literacy.

Summary

The model illustrates a solution for creating a viable financial literacy measuring program or tool. The construct necessary for the appropriate measurement of consumer's effective decision-making sustains actionable knowledge with the appropriate behaviors. The model provides practitioners and constituents with the proper mediums to perform actionable learning endeavors. These two actionable conditions allow the theory to lessen the gap, by filling the void with continuity, harnessing the precise motives to influence productive actions. These actions are important to leading a learning model that detects, and corrects an error, or inappropriate modes of motivation of existence in the financial literacy gap. (Holzmann, 2010, Huston, 2010)

Continuously replenishing the Financial Literacy gap requires the constant detection and correction of economic errors. The framework for the AFLDM includes Meta values of competence, self-efficacy, and religious purposes. (Argyris, 1996) This allows constituents to embrace a kinship to financial endeavors that are familiar with individual beliefs, organizational efforts, and a higher purpose. The leaders in the faith community understand that these Meta Values are key to the individual and significant to the faith-based community. As everyone improves financially then the group learns by collectively improving and creating an organization of financially astute believers.

This logical and spiritual interconnection is accepted as a viable theory for economic recreation to develop in an organization. (Argyris, 1996) The aim of the research endeavor was to create a very enriching and personally rewarding experience that positively changes financial literacy's influence on faith-based epistemology.

DR BLAKE'OLOGY

What does all this mean? I am not too sure? I know God wanted me to write this book. I studied, researched, and designed this book from the inside out. My goal was to have people tell me what they knew about financial stuff.

Now, I had to ask deep questions to get the ball rolling, yet I allowed the interviewee's to layout their insights in the responses. In many financial study's, researchers test one's knowledge about a product, a service, or a program.

This a presumption that individuals already have a preconceived understanding or knowledge about money concepts. My interests, is helping to create meaning, defining understanding, and adding to that body of knowledge. So, people can use the financial information they gain or that they already know.

I am just a brother
from the hood just trying
to Bmore good.

REFERENCES

Agle, B., & Van Buren III, H. (1999). God and mammon: The Modern Relationship. Business Ethics Quarterly, 9(4), 563-582. Retrieved November 7, 2010 from Business Source Complete database.

Anderson, G. (1988). Mr. Smith and the Preachers: The Economics of Religion in the Wealth of Nations. Journal of Political Economy, 96(5), 1066-1088. Retrieved December 3, 2010 from EconLit with Full text database.

Andrews, M., & Kacmer, K. (2001). Discriminating among organizational politics, justice, and support. Journal of Organizational Behavior, 22(4), 347-366. Retrieved September 22, 2010 from EBSCOhost database.

Angelides, P. (2011). The Financial Crisis Inquiry Report: Crisis was avoidable. The Financial Crisis Inquiry Commission. Washington, DC: Superintendent of Documents.

Arena, R., & Gloria-Palermo, S. (2008). Menger and Walras on Money: A Comparative View. History of Political Economy, 40(2), 317-343. Retrieved July 26, 2010 from ProQuest: ABI/INFORM Complete database.

Argyris, C. (1996). Actionable Knowledge: Design causality in the service of consequential theory. The Journal of Applied Behavioral Science, 32(4), 390-406.

Armstrong, P. (2001). Science, enterprising and profit: Ideology in the knowledge-driven economy. Economy and Society, 304(4), 523-552. Retrieved June 16, 2010 from EBSCOhost database.

Arnold, R. A. (1997). Economics. Cincinnati: South-Western College.

Avolio, B., & Yammariono, F. J. (2002). Transformational and Charismatic Leadership. (A. I. Science, Ed.)

Baker, B. (2007). A conceptual framework for making knowledge actionable through capital formation. Ann Arbor: ProQuest Information and Learning Company.

Barrett, F., & Peterson, R. (2000). Appreciative learning cultures: Developing competencies for global organizing. Organization Development Journal, 18(2), 10. Retrieved May 11, 2010 from EBSCOhost database.

Barro, R. J., & McCleary, R. M. (2003). Religion and Economic Growth across Countries. American Sociological Review, Vol.68, No. 5, 760-781. Retrieved December 6, 2010 from Business Source Complete database.

Baruch, E. (1999). Review of "Dispatches from eh Freud Wars: Psychoanalysis and its passions" and "Truth games: Lies, money and psychoanalysis". Psychoanalytic Psychology, 130-137. Retrieved January 10, 2011 form EBSCOhost database.

Becerra-Fernandez, I., Gonzalez, A., & Sabherwal, R. (2004). Knowledge Management. New Jersey: Prentice-Hall.

Belcher, J., & DeForge, B. (2007). Faith-Based Social Services. Journal of Religion and spirituality in social work, 26(4), 1, 1-19. Retrieved November 7, 2010 from Masterfile Premier database.

Beynon, M., & Maad, S. (2010). Empirical Modeling of Real-Life Financial Systems: The need for integration of enabling tools and technologies. Journal of Integrated Design and process Science, 6(1), 43.

Boulding, K. (1952). Religious Foundations of Economic Progress. Harvard Business Review, 33-40. Retrieved December 3, 2010 from Business Source Complete database.

Brainard, W., & Tobin, J. (1968). Pitfalls in Financial Model Building. American Economic Review, 58(2), 99-121. Retrieved July 13, 2010 from Business Source Complete Database.

Carlson, A. (2008). Discounting Family Values. American Conservative, 12-14. Retrieved July 27, 2010 from Academic Search Complete database.

Castaneda, R. R. (2004). Organizational financial literacy in a nonprofit organization. Ann Arbor: ProQuest Information and Learning Company.

Cochran, D., & Dolan, J. (1984). Qualitative Research: An alternative to Quantitative Research in Communication. Journal of Business Communication, 21(4), 25-32. Retrieved November 7, 2010 from Business Source Complete database.

Collins, J. M. (2010). Improving Financial Literacy: The role of non-profit providers. Pension Research Council, 1-32. Retrieved December 7, 2010 from Google Scholar database.

Cooper, D., & Schindler, P. (2003). Business research methods. Columbus: The McGraw-Hill.

Court, D. (2008). Qualitative Research as Cultural and Religious Mirror: What do Researchers Learn? Religious Education, 103(4), 410-426. Retrieved November 7, 2010 from the EBSCOhost database.

Cox, D. (2005). Good news! Behavioral economics is not going away anytime soon. The Journal of Product and Brand Management, 14 (6), 375 - 378.

Creswell, J. W. (2005). Educational Research: Planning, Conducting, and Evaluating Quantitative and Qualitative Research. Columbus: Merrill Prentice-Hall.

Dasgupta, P., & Maskin, E. (2005). Uncertainty and hyperbolic discounting. American Economic Review, 95(4), 1290-1299. Retrieved July 27, 2010 from Business Source Complete database.

Dent, H. (1998). The Roaring 2000s. New York: Simon & Schuster.

Drucker, P. (2008). Knowledge-Worker Productivity: The Biggest Challenge. California Management Review, 41(2), 79-94.

Education, F. R. (2004). Federal Reserve Bulletin, 90(4), 447-453. Washington D.C.: Board of Governors.

Estelami, H. (2009). Cognitive drivers of suboptimal financial decisions: Implications for financial literacy campaigns. Journal of Financial Services Marketing, 13(4), 273-283 Retrieved September 8, 2009. From Academic Search Complete database.

Fenneman, M., & Perkins, J. (2008). Mental budgeting versus marginal decision making: Training, experience and justification effects on decisions involving sunk cost. Journal of Behavioral Decision Making, 21(3), 225-239. Retrieved July 20, 2010 from EBSCOhost database.

Fitzpatrick, I., & Sagers, C. (2009). Faith-based financial regulation: A primer on oversight of credit rating organizations. Administrative Law, 61(3), 557-610.

Fulmer, R. J., & Keys, J. B. (2008). A conversation with Chris Argyris: the father of organizational learning. Organizational Dynamics 27n.2, 21-32. Retrieved July 1, 2010 from the EBCOhost database.

Gallagher, S., Rocco, T. S., & Landorf, H. (2007). A Direct experience study of spiritual and learning process at work: Exploring holistic theory of knowledge and learning. Human Resource Development Quarterly, 18 (4), 457 - 480.

Gerardi, K., & Willen, P. S. (2008). Subprime mortgages, Foreclosures, and Urban Neighborhoods. Research Review, 10 (6), 6 - 12.

Grebler, L. (1986). Household Saving in an Era of Financial Turmoil. Journal of Economic & Social Measurement, 14(2), 91-105. Retrieved November 3, 2010 from Business Source Complete database.

Groenwald, T. (2004). A direct experience research design illustrated. International Journal of Qualitative methods, 3 (2).

Harris, H. R. (2001, May). Joining faith and finance. Black Enterprise, 31 (10), p. 22.

Harris, K. (2001). Banks look at faith-based lending. ABA Banking Journal, 93 (9), 7 - 8.

Heath, T., Chatterjee, S., & France, K. (2010). Mental accounting and changes in price: The frame dependence of reference dependence. Journal of Consumer Research, 22(1), 90-97. Retrieved July 20, 2010 from Business Source Complete database.

Holzmann, R. (2010). Brining financial literacy and education to low- and middle-income countries. Pension Research Council, 1-21. Retrieved December 7, 2010 from Google Scholar database.

Hubbell, W. D. (2007). Assessing a customer service model in the financial service industry: A direct experience study. Ann Arbor: ProQuest information and Learning Company.

Huston, S. (2010). Measuring Financial Literacy. Journal of Consumer Affairs, 44(2), 296-316. Retrieved August 18, 2010 from EBSCOhost Database.

Johnson, M., Christensen, C., & Kagermann, H. (2008). Reinventing your business model. (cover story). Harvard Business Review, 86(12), 50-59. Retrieved August 13, 2010 from EBSCOhost database.

Jr., C. S. (1978). Financial planning with multiple objectives. Financial Management (1972), 7(4), 17-23. Retrieved July 13, 2010 from Business Source Complete database.

Kissane, R. (2007). How do faith-based organizations compare to secular providers? Nonprofit Directors' and Poor Women's' Assessments of FBO's. Journal of poverty, 11(4), 91-115. Retrieved November 7, 2010 from MasterFile Premier database.

Koonce, L. (1993). A Cognitive Characterization of Audit Analytical Review. Auditing, 57-76. Retrieved July 20, 2010 from Business Source Complete database.

Kopcke, R. W., Little, J. S., & Tootel, G. M. (2004). How Humans Behave: Implications for Economics and Economic Policy. New England Economic Review, 3 - 31.

Ladd, E. (1987). Secular and Religious America. Society, 24 (3), 63-68.

Lehrer, E. L. (2004). Religion as a determinant of economic and demographic behavior in the United States. IZA Discussion Paper Series No. 1390 (pp. 1-24). Chicago: University of Illinois at Chicago.

Lehrer, E. L. (2008). The role of religion in economic and demographic behavior in the United States: A review of recent literature. IZA Discussion Paper Series No. 3541 (pp. 1-24). Chicago: University of Illinois at Chicago.

Levav, J., & McGraw, A. (2009). Emotional Accounting: How Feelings About Money Influence Consumer Choice, 46(1), Journal of Marketing Research, 66-88. Retrieved July 20, 2010 from EBSCOhost database.

Lundby, K., & Rasinowich, C. (2003). The missing link. Market Research, 15(4), 14-19. Retrieved June 16, 2010 from Business Source Complete database.

Lusardi, A. (2008). Household Saving Behavior: The Role of Financial Literacy, Information, and Financial Education Programs. Dartmouth College and NBER.

Marinos, G. (2005). The information supply chain. DM Review, 15(4), 20-23. Retrieved June 16, 2010 from Business Source Complete database.

Mimbs-Johnson, C., & Lewis, A. (2009). Consumer economics and family resources: Importance of financial literacy. Journal of family & consumer sciences education, 27, 1-12. Retrieved September 8, 2009. from Education Research Complete database.

Neuman, W. L. (2003). Social Research Methods: Qualitative and quantitative approaches. 5th Ed. Boston: Pearson Education, Inc.

Nocetti, D. (2006). Hyperbolic Policymakers and Economic Growth. Economic Issues, 11(1), 41-48. Retrieved July 27, 2010 from Business Source Complete database.

Nonaka, I., & Nishiguchi, T. (2001). Knowledge Emergence. New York: Oxford University press.

Odean, T., & Simkins, B. (2008). An interview with Vernon L. Smith: 2002 Nobel Laureate in Economic Sciences and Father of Experimental Economics. Journal of Applied Finance, 18 (2), 116 - 123.

Office, C. B. (2006 йил 18-March). Congressional Budget Office. Retrieved 2010 йил 5-July from Congressional Budget Office: www.cbo.gov/showdoc.cfm?index=5195&sequence=0

Olson, D. T. (2009). The American Church in Crisis. Grand Rapids, MI, US: Zondervan.

Peifer, J. (2008). Serving God or Mammon? a look at religious mutual funds. American Sociological Association (pp. 1-21). American Sociological Association.

Presidential Committee on Information Literacy: Final Report. (1989). Washington, D.C.

Rachlin, H., Brown, J., & Cross, J. (2000). Discounting in Judgements of Delay and Probability. Journal of Behavioral Decision Making, 13(2), 145-159. Retrieved July 27, 2010 from Business Source Complete database.

Regency Bible. (1990). The Holy Bible. Thomas Nelson, Inc.

Schaefer, J., & Peluchette, J. (2010). Internal Control: Test your knowledge, 209(3), Journal of Accountancy, 46-49.

Schwandt, T. A. (2007). The Sage Dictionary of Qualitative Inquiry (Third ed.). Los Angeles, CA: Sage Publications, Inc.

Servon, L., & Kaestner, R. (2008). Consumer financial literacy and the impact of online banking on the financial behavior of lower-income bank customers. Journal of Consumer Affairs, 42(2), 271-305. Retrieved September 8, 2009 from Academic Search Complete database.

Slaughter, H. B. (2006). Financial Illiteracy: An American Epidemic. Ann Arbor: ProQuest Information and Learning Company.

Smith, P. (2008). Qualitative and Quantitative Research. Qualitative and Quantitative Research--Research Starters Education, 1, 1-9. Retrieved November 7, 2010 from Research Starters - Education database.

Soman, D., & Lam, V. M. (2002). The Effects of Prior Spending on Future Spending Decisions: The Role of Acquisition Liabilities and Payments. Hong Kong University of Science and Technology. Hong Kong: Kluwer Academic Publishers.

Stucke, M. (2009). Auditing Self-Interest. America, 201 (18), 10.

Stucke, M. E. (2009). Money, Is That What I Want? Competition Policy & the Role of Behavioral Economics. University of Tennessee Legal Studies Research. Santa Clara Law Review.

Thaler, R. (2008). Mental accounting and consumer choice. Marketing Science 27(1), 15-25. Retrieved July 20, 2010 from EBSCOhost database.

Thaler, R. (1999). Mental Accounting Matters. Journal of Behavioral Decision Making, 12(3), 183-206. Retrieved July 13, 2010 from Business Source Complete database.

Thomas, M. (2009). Faith and Collaboration: A Qualitative Analysis of Faith-Based Social Service Programs in Organizational Relationships. Administration in Social Work, 33(1), 40-60. Retrieved November 7, 2010 from MasterFile Premier database.

Tucker, M., Powell, K., & Meyer, G. (1995). Qualitative Research in Business Communication: A Review and Analysis. Journal of Business

Communication, 32(4), 383-399. Retrieved November 7, 2010 from Business Source Complete database.

US Census Bureau. (2011, August 27). The 2011 Statistical Abstract. Retrieved August 27, 27, from U.S. Census Bureau: www.census.gov/compendiastatab/cats/population/religion.html

USA Today Magazine. (2003, December). Faith Influences Wealth Accumulation. USA Today Magazine, 132 (16), 2303, 16. Valley Stream, NY, USA: USA Today.

White, D., & Lean, E. (2008). The impact of perceived leader integrity on subordinates in a work team environment. Journal of Business Ethics, 81 (4), 765-778.

Wiesen, J., & Carmichael, D. (1983). High Tech: A challenge for CPAs. Journal of Accountancy, 156(2), 67-72. Retrieved July 13, 2010 from Business Source Complete database.

Wolgemuth, L. (2008). Churches Are Preaching a New Gospel: Stay out of Debt. U.S. News & World Report, 144 (15), pp. 66 - 67.

Wuthnow, R. (2002). Religious involvement and status-bridging social capital. Journal for scientific study of religion, 41(4), 669-684. Retrieved December 7, 2010 from SocINDEX with Full Text database.

Wuthnow, R., Hackett, C., & Hsu, B. (2004). The effectiveness and trustworthiness of faith-based and other service organizations: A study of recipient's perceptions. Journal for Scientific Study of Religion, 43(1), 1-17. Retrieved July 1, 2010 from EBSCOhost database.

Wyk, K. V., & Ratliffe, C. (2007). Developing and marketing a faith-based practice: Mission and business. Journal of Psychology and Christianity, 26(3), 246-250. Retrieved August 12, 2010 from Academic Search Complete database.

Yi, R., Gatchalian, K., & Bickel, W. (2006). Discounting of past outcomes. Experimental and Clinical Psychopharmacology, 14(3), 311-317. Retrieved July 26, 2010 from EBSCOhost database.

APPENDIX A: INTERVIEW QUESTIONS

Section I: Demographics
Participant Status
1. How old are you
   a) 20 -30 b) 30 – 40 c) 50 – Mature Adult
2. Your Gender: Male or Female
3. Race/Ethnicity:
   a) African-American b) Asian c) Caucasian d) Hispanic
   e) Native Indian f) Other
4. Education:
   a) Graduate Degree b) Undergraduate Degree c) High-School d) Not-Finished High School
5. Marital Status:
   a) Married b) Divorced c) Widowed d) Single
6. Annual Income, Assets
   a) $25 - $35K b) 3$35 – 45K c) $45 - $50 d) $50 – Upper Income

Section II: Describe the level of perceived importance in relation to your current professional endeavors.

Logical Significance or Importance

1. What do you know about investments or investing in th market? Stocks, bonds, mutual funds, real estate, etc.?
2. What do you know and how important is life insurance?
3. What you know about fixed and variable interest?
4. What is the importance of a retirement plan?
5. How often do you read or study your religious text?
6. What is a credit score? How important is it?
7. What do you know about the Dow Jones? What does the Dow Jones do?
8. Which would you prefer $1,000 today or $10,000 in ten years?
9. How important is attending church services? Why?

Logical Progression or Actions Taken

Section III: Elaborate on your level of ability to perform the following actions in relations to your current financial endeavors.

1. How often do you read your investment statements? Stocks, bonds, mutual funds, or real estate's etc.?
2. What are the terms of your personal insurance policy?
3. What does the fine print on your credit card statement indicate?
4. What does it mean to fully fund a tax shelter? Example IRA or 401K?
5. What are the spiritual scriptures that you adhere to regarding money?
6. Do you have a financial professional? What written financial plans are you following and how often do you refer to its content?
7. Where is the Dow Jones now? What are your individual financial strategies?
8. What would you do with $100,000 after giving tithes and offerings?
9. How often do you attend, participate or visit your church?

APPENDIX B:
DATA COLLECTION TOOL

1 = Not at all, 2 = a slight extent, 3 = a moderate extent, 4 = great extent,
5 = mastery level

Financial Literacy

Logical Significance	Important
1. How well do you know investment?	1 2 3 4 5
2. How important is life insurance?	1 2 3 4 5
3. Rate your knowledge of fixed/variable interest?	1 2 3 4 5
4. Give the importance of a retirement plan?	1 2 3 4 5
5. How important is your credit score?	1 2 3 4 5

Logical Progression	Performance
1. Do you read your investment statements?	1 2 3 4 5
2. Did you read your personal insurance policy?	1 2 3 4 5
3. Read the fine print on credit card statements?	1 2 3 4 5
4. Do you fully fund your IRA?	1 2 3 4 5
5. Do you use a written financial plan & coach?	1 2 3 4 5

APPENDIX C: ANNOTATED
BIBLIOGRAPHY

Historical Overview and Current Findings
This report delved into the causes of the financial crisis that gripped the country and nearly collapsed the entire financial infrastructure. The commission members cite a lack on individual and societal responsibility as a primary contributor to the causes that plagued the system. A series of interconnected events contribute to on another compounding the magnitude of the ill-advised choices made by political as well as business leaders. These oversights lead to one of the most devastating economic upheavals besides the great depression with $11 trillion in household wealth disappearing and leaving 26 million people without a source of income.

Angelides, P (2011). The Financial Crisis Inquiry Report: Crisis was avoidable. PR Newswire. Retrieved January 30, 2011 from EBSCOhost database.

Chris Argyris is known as the father of organizational learning and his depiction of how companies learn to grow with individualism. Argyris exploits the accepted management theories and how predictable we implement actions in an unsurprising fashion. This can cause a stalemate in knowledge and has non-beneficial attributes on organizational growth. He believes companies can excel by creating memorable events that are theoretically and for people to implement.

Argyris, C. (2008). Actionable Knowledge: Design causality in the service of consequential theory. The Journal of Applied Behavioral Science, 32(4, 390-406.

This text discusses the role of Transformational Leadership as a catalyst for change in the environment in which it is relevant. The current state of leadership in the financial arena calls for a drastic change in the leadership philosophy. The text illustrated how monetary gain has less of an impact on performance than an appeal to integrity, honesty or authenticity.

Avolio, B. J., and Yammariono, F. J. (2002). Transformational and Charismatic Leadership. An Imprint of Elsevier Science.

To influence management, information technology integrates with an organizational strategy to effectively better managerial choices. The objective is making knowledge actionable through a systematic process of inquiry, description, and explanation into its effectiveness. Conceptualizing the role technology plays in accomplishing organizational goals and objectives is one of the starting points to understanding monetary growth.

Baker, B. A conceptual framework for making knowledge actionable through capital formation. D.Mgt. dissertation, University of Maryland University College, United States Maryland. Retrieved June 16, 2010, from ABI/INFORM Complete.

Appreciative learning cultures acknowledge the processes working well for an organization. The innovative insight allows for enhances performance by introducing new methods into the company. The fresh information ignites enthusiasm and empowers constituents to produce more. The economic future of organizations depends on individuals who thrive in appreciative learning cultures.

Barrett, F., and Peterson, R (2000). Appreciative learning cultures: Developing competencies for global organizing. Organization Development Journal, 18(2), 10. Retrieved May 11, 2010 from EBSCOhost database.

The article proposes a correlation between the success of a nation and the influence of its religious culture. Economic institutions are acutely affected by the religious beliefs of its culture and the religious elements that it serves. The author states, fostering economic progress stems from religious ethical contributions to capitalistic ideals.

Boulding, K (1952). Religious Foundations of Economic Progress. Harvard Business Review, 30(3), 33-40. Retrieved December 3, 2010 from Business Source Complete database.

The article emphasizes the need for a break from traditional research methodology, towards a modern theory of business communications. Within this structure sets the stage for researchers to display the significance of qualitative research to organizations as a viable means of establishing research truths.

Cochran, D., & Dolan, J. (1984). Qualitative Research: An Alternative to Quantitative Research in Communication. Journal of Business Communication, 21(4), 25-32. Retrieved November 7, 2010 from Business Source Complete database.

The Cooper text identifies the models necessary to accomplish sound qualitative and qualitative business research. Identifying the appropriate method and design requires a model congruent with the cognitive assessment of the research efforts.

Cooper, D., & Schindler, P. (2003). Business Research Methods. Columbus: The McGraw-Hill.

The article establishes the need for emotional content to be instilled in empirical research. The author addresses the need to gain more researchers' insights and to externalize thoughts to gain more understanding in cultural meanings. The process points to the research subjectivity that wrestles with the need to obtain an authentic voice on the research.

Court, D. (2008). Qualitative Research as Cultural and Religious Mirror: What Do Researchers Really Learn? Religious Education, 103(4), 410-426. Retrieved November 7, 2010 from the EBSCOhost database.

The Creswell text defines the parameters for completing a fundamentally sound academic research effort. The text outlines the procedures for conducting this qualitative study and illustrates the necessary factors to include in findings. The in-depth examination of the six-step process in the research process is instrumental in conducting this inquiry effort.

Creswell, J. W. (2005). Educational Research: Planning, Conducting, and Evaluating Qualitative and Qualitative Research. Columbus: Merrill Prentice-Hall.

The Drucker text identifies the role of the knowledge-worker in this technologically advanced economy. As constituents' transition and adapt in an environment becoming more complex, the knowledge-workers importance increases. Functioning in a financially literate world requires the expertise of a knowledge worker and demands that others begin to acquire skills to function in a digital society.

Drucker, P. (2008). Knowledge-Worker Productivity: The Biggest Challenge. California Management Review, 41(2), 79-94.

Chris Argyris further explains his 'Actionable Knowledge' as a method for leadership to evaluate priorities and evaluate its progress. He identified five series of questions each designed to aid the other in signifying where an organization stands and how to transform it into prolific action. R.J. Fulmer's conversation with Chris Argyris provides leaders with the essential attitudinal change elements to foster actionable behavior changes. The core elements of inquiry, explanatory, and descriptive mean to create opportunities outside of the original area experienced.

Fulmer, R. J., & Keys, J. B. (2008). A conversation with Chris Argyris: the father of organizational learning. Organizational Dynamics 27n.2.

The author indicates the thinking process involved with direct experience study and the in-depth perspective of the researcher. As the research efforts take shape there are three types of notes the researcher should maintain for a clear understanding. One should maintain observational notes on what are experiential, theoretical notes on meanings derived and methodological notes or critiques of the processes involved.

Groenewald, T. (2004). A direct experience research design illustrated. International Journal of Qualitative methods 3(2), Article 4. Retrieved Oct 2, 2010 from EBSCOhost database.

The Bible is a religious text that serves as the source of spiritual and emotional food for the faith-based constituent's soul or essence for being. The text provides a plethora of informational, educational, and practical knowledge for everyday living. Financial literacy for the faith-based constituent has its foundation, structure and belief system derived from this text.

James, K. (1990). The Holy Bible. Thomas Nelson, Inc.

This article depicts a means of developing a potential business model that begins with the customer as the initial focus. Financial literacy is found in educating the individual first and in turn corporate goals are obtain in conjunction with this endeavor. Creating value for the customer is that allows constituents to care for them self and their family. A successful organization creates a unique relationship between the services provided and product procured by loyal consumers.

Johnson, M., Christensen, C., & Kagermann, H. (2008). Reinventing your business model. (Cover story). Harvard Business Review, 86(12), 50-59. Retrieved August 13, 2010 from EBSCOhost database.

Religious affiliations affect the cost and benefits of the decisions people make over a lifetime. Religiosity influences economic outcomes because its accentuation of one's involvement in church activities. Religious values play a crucial role in fostering behaviors conducive to social and economic issues. Religiosity, beliefs and intellectual capital are variables measuring the factors pertinent to change behaviors.

Lehrer, Evelyn L., Religion as a Determinant of Economic and Demographic Behavior in the United States (November 2004). IZA Discussion Paper No. 1390. Retrieved December 7, 2010 from Google Scholar SSRN: http://ssrn.com/abstract=617413

The article synthesis religious influences on economic and demographic behavior based on beliefs and social affiliations. Important concepts derived from the article include the effects of wealth accumulation and investments in human capital. Socio-economic variables such as academic education play a vital role in the acquisition and understanding of financial endeavors.

Lehrer, Evelyn L., The Role of Religion in Economic and Demographic Behavior in the United States: A Review of the Recent Literature., Vol., pp. 1 - 24, Retrieved December 7, 2010

This text illustrated the effects as data progresses through its information channel in a fashion that influences actionable business knowledge and insight. This critical element pinpoints a potential methodology to explore and implement to effectively go beyond financial concepts via internal, external, and regulatory elements. The premise involves depicting a continuum of thought, knowledge, and wisdom to increase levels of connectedness and understanding.

Marinos, G. (2005). The Information Supply Chain. DM Review, 15(4), 20-23. Retrieved June 16, 2010 from Business Source Complete database.

This text provides the foundational information on conducting the appropriate scholarly research methodology. The author fully illustrates the necessary components of a qualitative research approach and supports the methodology. The proposed study will gain valuable insight into what scholarly needs are important to complete this research effort.

Neuman, W. L. (2003). Social Research Methods: Qualitative and qualitative approaches. 5th Ed. Boston: Pearson Education, Inc.

This text introduces the concept of "Ba" that refers shared space by two or more individuals or organizations, whether it is physical, virtual, and mental room. The realization of 'said' knowledge as a tangible element to effective leadership engineering is depicted in this text. The flow of information in "Ba" is anchored in the beliefs and commitment of constituents. This study's foundation is on influences of a belief system; this text helps constituents understand how to create financial knowledge out of knowledge.

Nonaka, I., & Nishiguchi, T. (2001). Knowledge Emergence. New York: Oxford University press.

The Presidential Committee has taken the strong stance on identifying how information literacy is a vital part of everyday life. As we continue along the expressway of the information super-highway, gaining access to this knowledge is necessary. A significant part of the report identified how the access and relevancy of gaining pertinent information is crucial to everyday survival.

Presidential Committee on Information Literacy: Final Report (1989). Washington, D.C.

The article proposes the research effort of a qualitative study holds more credence than a quantitative study. Qualitative studies are designs to discover, decide, and infer meaning that establishes meaningful theory. Reliability can provide proof by running mini-theories as the projects progresses along the research continuum. Furthermore, the skills of the analyst play a greater role in providing insight into consumerism from inferences established by a qualitative analyst.

Rossiter, J. (2008). Qualitative research rules. (pp. 915-919). World Advertising Research Center Limited. Retrieved November 7, 2010 from Business Source Complete database.

This text provides the fundamental precepts for qualitative inquiry that fulfills the academic rigors of valuable research. The author offers constructs of a researcher concentration on the phenomenology of the experience and how that experience constitutes everyday actions. In doing so, judgment about an existence suspends partiality allowing the researcher to focus on 'said' knowledge and its intrinsic involvement of the phenomenon.

Schwardt, T.A. (2007). The Sage Dictionary of Qualitative Inquiry (Third ed.) Los Angeles, CA: Sage Publications, Inc.

This article linked financial literacy with information technology and how this lack of access creates a deficiency in learning about finances. The article supports the claim of computer banking as an indicator for better financial shrewdness for its constituents. Disadvantage groups are less informed about mainstream financial matters and are computer illiterate are subject to the influence of technological advancement in the financial arenas.

This article gives great insight into the strengths and weaknesses of a qualitative and quantitative study. The author states that researcher's view how to exam the world and what is important in knowing the differences in discoveries. Qualitative research is based on an approach that draws its inference from the findings of the research and not from presumptions.

Smith, P. (2008). Qualitative & Quantitative Resecarci. Qualitative & Quantitative Research -- Research Starters Education, 1. Retrieved November 7, 2010 from Research Starters - Education database.

This foundational article depicts the cognitive behaviors that have permeated into the character traits of the average consumer. House adopts certain repetitive mental operations to keep track of financial activities. The advent of mental framing illustrates the value function, decision frames and hedonic framing. Simply, reframing references price adjustments as rebates rather than reduction to foster eagerness in a consumer's desire to make a purchase.

Thaler, R. (1999). Mental Accounting Matters. Journal of Behavioral Decision Making, 12(3), 183-206. Retrieved July 13, 2010 from Business Source Complete database.

This article discusses implicit or unsaid resolve employed by constituents and households to employ a mental accounting system. The article addresses the concept from a behavioral based theory explained in through three intricate features. One being a utility function expressed as value, and then cost is introduced through a function of reference price and finally the principle of fungibility.

Thaler, R. (2008). Mental Accounting and Consumer Choice. Marketing Science, 27(1), 15-25. Retrieved July 20, 2010 from EBSCOhost database. Doi: 10.1287/mksc.1070.0330.

This article illustrates the current and impending fate religious organizations deal with today because of the financial crisis. Religious organizations are suffering as donations have declined, membership attendance wanes, in a weak economic environment coupled with a high unemployment rate. The issue is that religious organizations to accommodate a growth there was a lack of a governing authority to address financial irregularities.

The Wall Street Journal. (2011, January 25).
Church foreclosures Surge, Seen as 'Next Wave' In Crisis.
The Wall Street Journal, p. 1.

This study explores business communications recognizing the phenomenon and generates interest in innovative research endeavors to define its meaning. The objective is to have practitioners seek to derive content of discovery more than justification. This approach allows for a greater understanding of social issues and identifies fundamental characteristics of a given phenomenon.

Tucker, M., Powell, K., & Meyer, G. (1995).
Qualitative Research in Business Communication:
A Review and Analysis. Journal of Business Communication,
32(4), 383-399. Retrieved November 7, 2010 from Business Source
Complete database.

The article emphasizes the awareness of corporate fraud and its cause for concern. The corrupt behavior witnessed over the past several years have generated interest in organizational activities. This increases the potential for scrutiny has created a sense of animosity toward the perceived integrity of corporate leaders.

White, D., & Lean, E. (2008). The impact of perceived
leader integrity on subordinates in a work team environment.
Journal of Business (81(4), 765-778.

Financial Literacy

The author describes three areas of organizational conflict relative to corporate as politics, justice, and support. Trust within an organization jeopardizes this type of illegitimate corporate behaviors are in operation. Member conflict is inevitable and organizational learning begins to suffer from this dilemma that hinders productivity. This report recognizes the importance of organizational learning and if economic learning is affected the bottom–line becomes stagnate.

Andrews, M., & Kacmar, K. (n.d). Discriminating among
organizational politics, justice, and support. Journal of
Organizational Behavior, 22(4), 347-366. Retrieved September 22,
2010 from EBSCOhost database. Doi: 10.1002/job.92.

This article provides interesting insights into the monetary exchange process experienced by the consumer. The refinement of money being money as its relevance becomes the preferred and historical development of people who trade. The judgments of constituents economize its importance and assigns value to the essential need for exchange.

Arena, Richard and Gloria-Palermo, Sandye, G. (n.d). Menger and Walras on Money: A Comparative View. History of Political Economy, 40(2), 317. Retrieved July 26, 2010 from ProQuest: ABI/INFORM Complete database.

This brief article identifies the fears of middle-class Americans toward the moral and social decay of society. These premises could prove valuable in identifying factors that diminish the perceived value of obtaining an object. Consumer's 'said' knowledge guides the more than explicit resolve, and base important decisions on its moral or social responsibility.

Carlson, A. (2008, November 17). Discounting Family Values. American Conservative, pp. 12-14. Retrieved July 27, 2010 from Academic Search Complete database.

This dissertation emphasizes the importance of organizational financial literacy and its influence on corporate financial performance and employee readiness. The research revealed financially literate employees relied more on over time for survival and less on optimizing regular labor hours. Constituents who were astute in personal financial endeavors contributed effectively to the corporate bottom-line.

Castaneda, R. R. (2004). Organizational financial literacy in a nonprofit organization. Ann Arbor: ProQuest Information and Learning Company.

This report illustrated the federal governments interest in ensuring all Americans in obtaining a pertinent financial education. The Federal Reserve highlighted the need for individuals to make sound financial decisions and raise the awareness of available financial educational resources. Ideally, individuals need to be aware avoiding high-cost debt, comparison shopping for credit and understanding credit history. These are financial matters the federal government had not been known for indulging in.

Education, F. R. (2004). Federal Reserve Bulletin, 90(4), 447-453. Washington D.C.: Board of Governors.

This text provides the means to illustrate pertinent traits illustrated in the research portion of this study. The study identifies essential traits harbored by the average consumer that causes constituents to forgo rational behaviors, despite obvious financial perils. The context of the article identified areas of economic significance that individuals perceive as unimportant or lesser economic value.

Estelami, H. (2009). Cognitive drivers of suboptimal financial decisions: Implications for financial literacy campaigns. Journal of Financial Services Marketing, 13(4), 273-283 Retrieved September 8, 2009. From Academic Search Complete database.

The article illustrates how constituents ignore sunken cost information and consequently make irrational monetary decisions. Investing the stock market weighs heavily on this alluring precept in which would be investor's use as a rationale for not investing. Individuals lose the potential for gain when they do not take part in a process that could yield them a windfall.

Fennema, M., & Perkins, J. (2008). Mental budgeting versus marginal decision-making: training, experience and justification effects on decisions involving sunk costs. Journal of Behavioral Decision Making 21(3), 225-239 Retrieved July 20, 2010 from EBSCOhost database. Doi: 10.1002/bdm.585.

In this article the author illustrates the turmoil that occurring during a recessionary period like events occurring from 2001- 2010. The article attempts to highlight savings behaviors in correlation to measuring consumer savings. It is interesting that the article attributes unparalleled events of that time to the Great Depression. A great amount of uncertainty lingered on the hearts and minds of the average consumer to the degree that spending curtails.

Grebler, L. (1986). Household Saving in an Era of Financial Turmoil, 1975--1984. Journal of Economic & Social Measurement,

14(2), 91-105. Retrieved November 3, 2010 from Business Source
Complete database.

This text provides empirical evidence on the significance of birth and spending cycles that influence the economic structure of the monetary system. Most of this text applies financial spending patterns against birth, grow, and expansion periods of specific people groups. The author depicts how the 'Baby-boomer' generation have played an intricate role in grow and expansion of the economic explosion turned implosion in the United States.

Harry S. Dent, J. (1998). The Roaring 2000s.
New York: Simon & Schuster

The crux of this article centers on two principles: diminishing marginal sensitivity and loss aversion. Consumers frequently grapple with the two principles in pursuit of financial decision. The reasoning yields four principles for maximizing values:

1. Segregated multiple gains (two gains),
2. Integrate mixed gains (again with a smaller loss),
3. Integrated multiple losses (two losses),
4. Segregated mixed losses (a loss with a smaller gain)

(Heath, Chatterjee, & France, 2010, p. 90).\

These principles prove the disparity faced by constituents when seeking to make a favorable financial decision.

Heath, T., Chatterjee, S., & France, K. (1995). Mental
Accounting and Changes in Price: The Frame Dependence of
Reference Dependence. Journal of Consumer Research, 22(1),
90-97. Retrieved July 20, 2010 from Business Source
Complete database.

Highlights of this article are two key activities implemented to measure financial literacy in low and middle-income countries. Financial literacy is consequently a global challenge whereby leaders of countries are focusing on educating its countryman. Also, the research illustrates the results of the causal influence of financial educational and other intervention efforts. A common theme across a global perspective calls for an individual to understand financial matters; this is good for the individual and global economics. The article further defines what it means to be a financially capable individual.

Holzmann, Robert, Bringing Financial Literacy and Education to Low- and Middle-Income Countries (November 11, 2010). Pension Research Council WP 2010-38. Retrieved December 7, 2010 from Google Scholar SSRN: http://ssrn.com/abstract=1707673

The direct experience study focused on the financial services industry's adoption of the "Three-C's" model. Competence, compliance, and courtesy are the guideposts for this research effort to further refine the ethical practices for debt collectors. The study included seven principles for conducting qualitative interviews. The study serves as a model on approaching the proposed financial literacy study.

Hubbell, W. Assessing a customer service model in the financial services industry: A direct experience study. D.M. dissertation, University of Phoenix, United States -- Arizona. Retrieved August 19, 2010, from Dissertations & Theses @ University of Phoenix. (Publication No. AAT 3302618).

This article provides a solution for creating a viable financial literacy measuring program or tool. The author posits that a construct is necessary for the appropriate measurement of consumer's effective decision making. The article provides research with a preliminary glimpse at an Actionable Financial Literacy model for practitioners and constituents to implement as the proper mediums to perform actionable financial learning endeavors evolve.

Huston, S. (2010). Measuring Financial Literacy. Journal of Consumer Affairs, 44(2), 296-316. Retrieved August 18, 2010 From EBSCOhost Database doi:10.1111/j.1745-6606.2010.01170.x.

The author illustrates how individual behaviors change and personal circumstances alter one's life direction. This phenomenon undermines the consistency causing indifference in the context of financial concepts. Herein lays a need to refine elements of fairness, economic utility and the welfare of constituency. This expresses the need for social researchers to develop a model that can be applicable to intuitive aspects of actionable financial literacy.

Richard W Kopcke, Jane Sneddon Little,
& Geoffrey M B Tootell. (2004). How Humans Behave:
Implications for Economics and Economic Policy.
New England Economic Review, 3-31. Retrieved August 19, 2010,
from ABI/INFORM Global. (Document ID: 682607991).

This dissertation depicts the inabilities of the family unit to create fundamental financial educations to young African American teens. The limited knowledge of economic matters resulted in 42.3 % of family's net worth to debt. The article depicted a cycle of financial illiteracy permeating from a young adulthood, to middle age and then to senior citizenship.

Slaughter, H. B. (2006). Financial Illiteracy: An American
Epidemic. Ann Arbor: ProQuest Information and Learning
Company.

This article emphasizes a reexamination of current economic theory pertaining to self-interest, considering the fall-out from the financial crisis. The current theory of self-interest being the catalyst and a contributing factor for the failure of big business, a need for change has arisen. The author recommends self-interest is mediated with an understanding of human behavior as the cornerstone to economic growth.

Stucke, M. E. (2009). Auditing Self-Interest. America,
201(18), 10. Retrieved April 4, 2011 from EBSCOhost database.

This article illustrates the widening income gap in the US, the author points to trends established and in comparison, to the 1970s. In the article the central theme describes how self-interest and irregular desires can collectively lead to economic catastrophe. The author seeks a governing resolve to promote the acquisition of capital in comparative terms. This article enhances this study by providing probable insight into the thought process of individuals seeking financial knowledge.

Stucke, Maurice E., Money, Is That What I Want? Competition
Policy & the Role of Behavioral Economics (June 14, 2009).
University of Tennessee Legal Studies Research Paper No. 75;
Santa Clara Law Review, Vol. 50, 2010. Retrieved April 4, 2011
from Google Scholar SSRN database.

As organizations steer toward a profitable future traditional industry are finding research and development practices in technology obsolete. Accounting issues have highlighted the need to procure accurate data to report to the Securities and Exchange Commission. This revelation pinpoints the necessity of technological supremacy in the financial arena.

Wiesen, J., & Carmichael, D. (1983). HIGH TECH: A CHALLENGE FOR CPAS. Journal of Accountancy, 156(2), 67-72. Retrieved July 13, 2010 from Business Source Complete database.

Faith-Based Epistemology
The author states that attending religious services influences constituent's tendency to build wealth. A member draws upon religion to develop strategies and plans to address proper stewardship of wealth accumulation. For instance, Jews amass a considerable amount of wealth compared to other belief groups.

Faith Influences Wealth Accumulation. (2003). USA Today Magazine, 132(2703) 16. Retrieved December 3, 2010 from Masterfile Premier database.

This Article connects economics and religion as an intertwining phenomenon. Religion influences social behaviors that correlate into wealth creation. As perceptions of personal character influence the expectations of the individual his or her expected income increases accordingly.

Anderson, G. (1988). Mr. Smith and the Preachers: The Economics of Religion in the Wealth of Nations. Journal of Political Economy, 96(5), 1066-1088. Retrieved December 3, 2010 from EconLit with Full Text database.

This article correlates the significance of Christian beliefs and its linkage to economic prosperity, a cultural phenomenon. The assertion that value systems come from a dominant culture and influences Faith-Based Organizations (FBOs) who claim a prophetic role for monetary success. Corporate Social Responsibility was also explored to determine the differences religious upbringing; practices or beliefs affect cognitive behaviors.

Agle, B., & Van Buren III, H. (1999). GOD AND MAMMON: THE MODERN RELATIONSHIP. Business Ethics Quarterly, 9(4), 563-582. Retrieved November 7, 2010 from Business Source Complete database.

The article depicts the causation of religiosity on economic performance resulting in church attendance and belief variables. The authors imply empirical evidence supporting religious beliefs to positive economic occurrences. The individual behaviors derived from the principle output of beliefs and church attendance signifies a potential increase GDP and in personal resources.

Barro, R. J., & McCleary, R. M. (2003). Religion and Economic Growth across Countries. American Sociological Review, Vol.68, No. 5, 760-781. Retrieved December 6, 2010 from Business Source Complete database.

The article depicts how social reality constructs properly determine the worthiness of those seeking services from FBOs. A qualitative approach is put in place to establish the perceive level of service received by participants. The article undertakes the task of monitoring judgment and why people behave the way they do.

Belcher, J., & DeForge, B. (2007). Faith-Based Social Services: The Challenges of Providing Assistance. Journal of Religion & Spirituality in Social Work, 26(4), 1. Retrieved November 7, 2010 from Masterfile Premier database.

Collins emphasizes the role of nonprofit organizations in providing solutions to common money challenges and raising the awareness for financial literacy. Low income and minorities are key people groups that are more likely to take advantage of the programs offered by nonprofit agencies. Typically, nonprofit organizations are not profit-driven, having no vested interest in consumers' financial choices. This premise presumes constituents will receive information relevant to their situation rather than being won over to make a purchase.

Collins, J. Michael, (2010). Improving Financial Literacy: The Role of Nonprofit Providers (November 11, 2010). Pension Research Council WP 2010-39. Retrieved December 7, 2010 from Google Scholar SSRN: http://ssrn.com/abstract=1707674

This article depicts the responsibilities of credit rating organizations (CROs) and the irregularity of the corporate ratings for profit. The question of the strength and accuracy in the reporting has caused concerns as the economic crisis ensues. Financial markets and individuals bear the brunt of the ill advises ratings of substandard corporations.

Fitzpatrick, I., & Sagers, C. (2009). FAITH-BASED FINANCIAL REGULATION: A PRIMER ON OVERSIGHT OF CREDIT RATING ORGANIZATIONS. Administrative Law Review, 61(3), 557-610. Retrieved June 29, 2010 from Business Source Complete database.

The author illustrates the influences of spirituality in adult cognitive assessments during the learning experience. Ethical and moral actions contrived by personal convictions could prove beneficial to organizational endeavors. Creativity enhanced by a vibrant learning experience evolves from constituents who add spirituality to the educational process. Faith-based learning and teachings regarding financial literacy could benefit from these resolves.

Gallagher, S.J., Rocco, T.S., & Landorf, H. (Winter 2007). A Direct experience study of spiritual and learning process at work: Exploring holistic theory of knowledge and learning. Human Resource Development Quarterly, Vol. 18, no.4, 457-480. Retrieved November 4, 2010 from EBSCOhost database.

This text illustrates the intent of religious leaders to educate their members in financial literacy. The author discusses the intent of the Rainbow/Push organization's efforts to commit 1,000 churches to teaching and educating its members about money. The literacy program desires to educate consumers on the science of capital and debt, investing and home ownership.

Harris, H. (2001). Joining faith and finance. Black Enterprise, 31(10), 22. Retrieved June 29, 2010 from Academic Search Complete database.

The article depicts efforts of Faith-Based Organizations (FBO) and several credit unions banks in creating programs to help achieve financial dreams. The author suggests that individuals who 'pray' develop a more resounding resolve to 'pay', other constituents. The Faith-Based

Lending Act guided initiatives to bring together 250 churches in the Washington D.C. area focused on community development.

Harris, Kaisha (2001). Banks look at faith-based lending. American Bankers Association. ABA Banking Journal, 93(9), 7-8. Retrieved August 19, 2010, from ABI/INFORM Global. (Document ID: 81508384).

FBOs have been suggest and backed by policy makers to increase their role in providing services to the local communities. The article highlighted four key areas where FBOs differ in rendering services; individualized care, religiosity in service, community affiliations and professionalism. These differences serve as a catalyst to raise the expectation levels on constituents on the lower end of the economic spectrum.

Kissane, R. (2007). How Do Faith-Based Organizations Compare to Secular Providers? Nonprofit Directors' and Poor Women's Assessments of FBOs. Journal of Poverty, 11(4), 91. Retrieved November 7, 2010 from Masterfile Premier database.

This research document introduces the thought of a religious foundation established in technologically advanced nations. The United States is unique in that comprises both elements of being a religious nation and a prominent technological advanced country. The combination of the two-character traits are not found in other nations and thus caused the study efforts.

Ladd, E. C. (1987). Secular and Religious America. Society, Mar/Apr87, Vol. 24 Issue 3,63-68 Retrieved December 3, 2010 from Masterfile Premier database.

This conference paper illuminates socially responsible investing (SRI), a concept influenced by religion. The model is the precursor of religious mutual fund investing that adheres to the religious beliefs of the proposed investor. Socially, a screening or "Sin Screening" investment choice has become the preferred method to avoid industries such as tobacco, alcohol, and military armament.

Peifer, J. (2008). Serving God or Mammon? A look at religious mutual funds. Conference Papers - American Sociological Association, 1. Retrieved December 3, 2010 from SocINDEX with Full Text database.

This research article exhorts how religious organizational members are increasingly relying upon the congregational entity to provide more social services. In faith-related organizations 75% of 193 agencies studied access financial resources on the behalf of their constituents and 66% used the facilities of the local congregations for various purposes. The need for representatives of faith-based organizations to acquire expert knowledge increases as demands for social services continues to rise.

Thomas, M. (2009). Faith and Collaboration: A Qualitative Analysis of Faith-Based Social Service Programs in Organizational Relationships. Administration in Social Work, 33(1), 40. Retrieved November 7, 2010 from Masterfile Premier database.

The article emphasizes the difficulties of integrating one's faith as the guidepost to clinically managing organizational endeavors. This innovative approach appeals to the current trend of developing business models not driven by bottom-line profits. Assessing the current perspective of an organization could yield pertinent insight to building an organizations success built upon a belief system. Passion, ability, support and mission are held as the driving force of current corporate endeavors.

Van Wyk, K., & Ratliffe, C. (2007). Developing and Marketing a Faith-Based Practice: Mission and Business. Journal of Psychology & Christianity, 26(3), 246-250. Retrieved August 12, 2010 from Academic Search Complete database.

The article comments on hindrances to the ability of its member's spiritual growth by illogical relationship constituents have with money. Constituents seek financial advice from theologians to combat issues of want to hoard money, being a spend thrifts or experience debt bondage. The author depicts a concentrated effort to reach the younger 20 something generation who have a sense of lethargy regarding money.

Wolgemuth, L. (2008). Churches Are Preaching a New Gospel: Stay out of Debt. U.S. News & World Report, 144(15), 66-67 Retrieved March 28, 2010 from EBSCOhost database.

This literary piece sheds light on the correlations between religious involvement and building social capital. Economic influence is an unlikely result of this interesting relationship within the context these unique religious interactions. Social relationships can help constituents acquire influence through which one could advance economically by securing suitable employment. The people, who congregate in religious circles, as mentioned in the article, are individuals with potential influence and connections that can provide opportunity to others.

Wuthnow, R. (2002). Religious Involvement and Status-Bridging Social Capital. Journal for the Scientific Study of Religion, 41(4), 669-684. Retrieved December 7, 2010 from SocINDEX with Full Text database.

This article depicts the importance of faith-based organizations in the scope of providing services to individuals. In the article the author remarks on a statement by former President Bush, "Charities and faith based groups till needs that no welfare system, no matter how well designed, can possibly fill...in times of personal crisis, people do not need the rules of a bureaucracy; they need the help of a neighbor" (Wuthnow, 2004, pg. 1). The importance of faith-based organizational leaders to provide a vital role in the financial lives of others is greater now than ever before.

Wuthnow, R., Hackett, C., & Hsu, B. (2004). The Effectiveness and Trustworthiness of Faith-Based and Other Service Organizations: A Study of Recipients' Perceptions. Journal for the Scientific Study of Religion, 43(1), 1-17. Retrieved July 1, 2010 from EBSCOhost database.

Behavioral Economics

Armstrong, P. (2001). Science, enterprise and profit: ideology in the knowledge-driven economy.

Economy & Society, 30(4), 524-552. Retrieved June 16, 2010 from ESBCOhost database. doi:10.1080/03085140120089081.

R.A. Arnold details the pertinent lessons for macro and microeconomics as depicted throughout this dissertation. Arnold illustrated the context of buyer behavior while providing the means for quantifying 'said' behaviors. The fundamental principles outlined in this text provide key insights into the monetary factors contributing to the mindset of the consumer. These principles could translate into faith-based nomenclature and understood by constituents.

Arnold, R. A. (1997). Economics. Cincinnati: South-Western College.

The article gives an instinctive resolve to lies and deceit, which are traits prevalent in the culture of money. A Freudian influence of psychoanalysis illuminates how culturally lying is an innate virtue for people to preserve themselves. The truth is merely an illusion or a metaphor that is a result of habitual behaviors. This assumption can transcend insight into causes of recurrent financial misgivings or perpetual economic miscalculations.

Baruch, E. (1999). Review of "Dispatches from the Freud wars: Psychoanalysis and its passions" and" Truth games: Lies, money and psychoanalysis". Psychoanalytic Psychology, 16(1), 130-137. Retrieved Jan 10, 2011 from EBSCOhost database.

This text introduces a learning model of 'said' knowledge as means of increasing the understanding of learning. Explicit knowledge has its value, however, can require more rigorous statures for others to accept as authentic and valid. The premise is to find which learning model is most proficient in learning and applying financial literacy.

Becerra-Fernandez, I., Gonzalez, A., & Sabherwal, R. (2004). Knowledge Management. New Jersey: Prentice-Hall.

This article illustrates technology's accelerated influence on business in general and the financial industry. Organizations are changing and the effect of innovative changes alters corporate efficiencies in an unpredictable and risky fashion. The implementation of financial analysis tools into the infrastructure of cyber-learning ineffective when compared to unforeseen economic factors.

Beynon, M., & Maad, S. (2002). EMPIRICAL MODELING OF REAL-LIFE FINANCIAL SYSTEMS: THE NEED FOR INTEGRATION OF ENABLING TOOLS AND TECHNOLOGIES.

Journal of Integrated Design & Process Science, 6(1), 43. Retrieved July 13, 2010 from Academic Search Complete database.

These authors who relate functions of assets and debts discussed the complexities of financial market. Ideally, computer simulations of a fictitious economy could develop capture 'said' and explicit knowledge in financial literacy. One of the most influential statements made by the authors was, "You can't get something for nothing".

Brainard, W., & Tobin, J. (1968). PITFALLS IN FINANCIAL MODEL BUILDING. American Economic Review, 58(2), 99. Retrieved July 13, 2010 from Business Source Complete database.

Behavioral economics illustrates the preferences of consumerism that does not require actions to be rational. Choices based on what's fashionable and preferable balance by logic and evidence with the ability to predict behaviors. Current economic research recognizes brand loyalty, acceptance, and welcomes as the guidepost for acquiring the astute consumer.

Cox, Donald (2005). Good news! Behavioral economics is not going away anytime soon. The Journal of Product and Brand Management, 14(6), 375-378. Retrieved August 19, 2010, from ABI/INFORM Global. (Document ID: 974622831).

Dasgupta and Maskin, compare the similarities of animals and humans regarding economic or behavioral ecology toward future versus present goals. The discoveries of the articles support consumers becoming less patient with an endeavor even when the success is about to happen. The study further stipulated that one's preferences shape our behaviors because of evolutionary forces. Conventional wisdom provided by economics suggests when future windfalls appear uncertain its present value diminishes.

Dasgupta, P., & Maskin, E. (2005). Uncertainty and Hyperbolic Discounting. American Economic Review, 95(4), 1290-1299. Retrieved July 27, 2010 from Business Source Complete database.

This article explains the disproportionate amount of foreclosures amount minorities. As the rapid growth home ownership expanded, this form of lending took place in minority and low-income communities. The author places the emphasis on lenders and calls for procedures to introduce principal reduction methods.

Gerardi, K. S., & Willen, P. S. (2008). Subprime Mortgages, Foreclosures, and Urban Neighborhoods. Research Review, (10), 6. Retrieved January 22, 2011 from EBSCOhost database.

Audit Analysis encompasses identifying root causes in financial relationships and account fluctuations. The purpose of the article was to embark on a cognitive journey to address review as diagnostic, sequential, and iterative processing. Ideally the task performed was to address the psychological ability to successfully represent audit challenges.

Koonce, L. (1993). A Cognitive Characterization of Audit Analytical Review. Auditing, 12(2), 57. Retrieved July 20, 2010 from Business Source Complete database.

This article detailed description between mental accountings and emotional accounting redefined the endeavor to explicate finances. Emotional accounting context derives from 'said' knowledge and feelings evoke in the process of spending money. The article depicts the values derived and the intensity of the feeling exerted toward the object referred to as money.

Levav, J., & Mcgraw, A. (2009). Emotional Accounting: How Feelings About Money Influence Consumer Choice. Retrieved July 20, 2010 from Journal of Marketing Research (JMR), 46(1), 66-80. doi:10.1509/jmkr.46.1.66.

Employee engagement and service orientation influences customer loyalty and affects corporate revenues. Cohorts, who understand the cause and effect relationship between differing organizational metrics, can bolster organizational efforts to achieve goals. Therefore, understanding the financial aspect of corporate operation in line with personal endeavors can garner needed support for the company's agenda.

Lundby, K., & Rasinowich, C. (2003). The missing link. Marketing Research, 15(4), 14-19. Retrieved June 16, 2010 from Business Source Complete database.

The article suggests using empirical data to promote the need for financial literacy across the United States. An acute need exists for financial literacy, especially among low-income groups, African-American and Hispanics. Expected utility measured consumer's expectations over a lifetime and the difficulty of making savings decisions.

Lusardi, Annamaria, Household Saving Behavior: The Role of Financial Literacy, Information, and Financial Education Programs (February 2008). Retrieved August 18, 2010 From EBSCOhost Database NBER Working Paper No. W13824. Available at SSRN: http://ssrn.com/abstract=1094290

This article provides the numerical values specific to a family's problematic spending behavior. Ideally, to illustrate the shortcomings of the individual versus understanding the purpose behind purchasing habits is the prevalent point of this article. The author discusses teaching the skill of properly using resources and developing competencies in financial literacy. Distinctively, the objective is to define processes to gaining knowledge and an effective skill set to manage resources versus altering behaviors that influence consumer choices.

Mimbs-Johnson, C., & Lewis, A. (2009). Consumer economics and family resources: Importance of financial literacy. Journal of family & consumer sciences education, 27, 1-12. Retrieved September 8, 2009. from Education Research Complete database.

This article linked the actions of politicians in officer who place more emphasis on current rather than his or her future outcomes to hyperbolic discounting. In the political economic literature arena decision making at times appears to be focused on today without a concern for the future. The concept of time-preference introduction into the role of policy making could effectively increase the validity of decision makers.

Nocetti, D. (2006). Hyperbolic Policymakers and Economic Growth. Economic Issues, 11(1), 41-48. Retrieved July 27, 2010 from Business Source Complete database.

The interview expounds on the fundamentals of decision-making, decision-making under uncertainty, and other related issues. The articles understanding of market mechanisms and the influences of behavioral financial economics are spoken about. Models of fundamentalist and momentum traders helped identify bubbles we observed in asset trading.

Odean, T., & Simkins, B. (2008). An Interview with Vernon L. Smith: 2002 Nobel Laureate in Economic Sciences and Father of Experimental Economics. Journal of Applied Finance, 18(2), 116-123. Retrieved August 19, 2010, from ABI/INFORM Global. (Document ID: 1709766201).

The CBO grants new federal regulatory control and authority to organizations to reduce the probability of another severe financial crisis. An element of financial literacy involves addressing inconsistencies within the structure of financial firms. The securities market is an area of substantial gain for constituents but also an area subject to misguiding by unethical leaders.

Office, C. B. (2006, March 18). Congressional Budget Office. Retrieved July 5, 2010, from Congressional Budget Office: www.cbo.gov/showdoc.cfm?index=5195&sequence=0

The options of choices we make are not always equally probable or occur at the same time. A delay in receiving such a reward depends on its relevant size, e.g. the smaller the reward the longer the delay. Delayed rewards correspond or imply uncertainty and could indicate that its causes are problematic. Also, the less likely a reward is to be received the longer the delay.

Rachlin, H., Brown, J., & Cross, D. (2000). Discounting in Judgments of Delay and Probability. Journal of Behavioral Decision Making, 13(2), 145-159. Retrieved July 27, 2010 from Business Source Complete database.

This article discusses internal controls as a process design for business owners to control expenditures and achieve optimal efficiency. Also, the article covers the desire to understand corporate risk management and the need to avoid perils of mismanaging organizational endeavors. In a questionnaire format, the author submits the use of a code-of conduct to be the source of guiding behaviors.

Schaefer, J., & Peluchette, J. (2010). Internal Control: Test Your Knowledge. Journal of Accountancy, 209(3), 46-49. Retrieved June 16, 2010 from Business Source Complete database.

The content of this literary piece focuses on the subjectivity and preferences rendered in monetary decision-making. In this discussion the assumption that organizations seek wealth maximization primarily rather than multiple objectivity of corporate endeavors. The model implemented to measure these distinctions channeled its thoughts on utility-maximizing solutions. Values chosen by constituents examine the efficiency of the solutions established to resolve preferences.

Sealey Jr., C. (1978). Financial Planning with Multiple Objectives. Financial Management (1972), 7(4), 17-23. Retrieved July 13, 2010 from Business Source Complete database.

Two distinct episodes measure spending habits, acquisition liability episode and payment episode. Acquisition liability episodes equate to the making a purchase that commits individuals to allocating future resources to acquire goods and services. Payment episodes actualize the depletion of wealth when consumers pay credit cards and other debit instruments on a consistent basis.

Soman, Dilip & Lam, Vivian M. W. (2002). The Effects of Prior Spending on Future Spending Decisions: The Role of Acquisition Liabilities and Payments. Marketing Letters, 13(4), 359. Retrieved August 19, 2010, from ABI/INFORM Global. (Document ID: 331767431).

A time reference in this article pertains to special and social distance about past temporal distance. The relevance of positive outcomes (gains) are being discounted more so than the negative outcome (losses) is depicted in the article. Furthermore, the article illustrates hyperbolic equations where relative decline in value decreases as delay in obtaining a gain increase.

Yi, R., Gatchalian, K., & Bickel, W. (2006). Discounting of past outcomes. Experimental and Clinical Psychopharmacology, 14(3), 311-317. Retrieved July 23, 2010 from EBSCOhost database. doi:10.1037/1064-1297.14.3.311.

APPENDIX D:
SURVEY RESULTS

Constant Contact Survey Results

Survey Name: Financial Literacy Research Combined

Response Status: Partial & Completed

Filter: None

8/12/2012 11:39 AM MST

✻Rate your level of significance or importance regarding the following subjects?

1 = Not at all, 2 = Slightly, 3 = Moderately, 4 = Greatly, 5 = Mastery level

Answer	1	2	3	4	5	Number of Response(s)	Rating Score*
How well do you know investments?						30	2.5
How important is life insurance?						30	3.7
Rate your knowledge of fixed/variable interest?						30	2.9
Give the importance of a retirement plan?						30	3.8
How important is your credit score?						30	4.0

*The Rating Score is the weighted average calculated by dividing the sum of all weighted ratings by the number of total responses.

1 = Not at all, 2 = Slightly, 3 = Moderately, 4 = Greatly, 5 = Master Level

Answer	1	2	3	4	5	Number of Response(s)	Rating Score*
Do you read your investment statements?						30	2.4
Did you read your personal insurance policy?						30	2.8
Read the fine print on credit card statements?						30	2.7
Do you fully fund your IRA/401K?						30	2.3
Do you use a written plan and coach?						30	1.8

*The Rating Score is the weighted average calculated by dividing the sum of all weighted ratings by the number of total responses.

JOSEPH - BUILDING FINANCIAL LITERACY

*What is your gender?

Answer	0%	100%	Number of Response(s)	Response Ratio
Male			17	56.6 %
Female			13	43.3 %
No Response(s)			0	0.0 %
		Totals	30	100%

*What is your age?

Answer	0%	100%	Number of Response(s)	Response Ratio
20 - 30			4	13.3 %
31- 40			7	23.3 %
41 - 50			9	30.0 %
51 - Mature Adult			10	33.3 %
No Response(s)			0	0.0 %
		Totals	30	100%

*What best describes your race or ethnicity?

Answer	0%	100%	Number of Response(s)	Response Ratio
African-American			9	30.0 %
Asian			0	0.0 %
Caucasian			5	16.6 %
Hispanic/Latino			12	40.0 %
Native American			0	0.0 %
other			1	3.3 %
Other			3	10.0 %
No Response(s)			0	0.0 %
		Totals	30	100%

*Which of the following categories best describes your annual income?

Answer	0%	100%	Number of Response(s)	Response Ratio
$25,000 - $35,000			15	50.0 %
$36,000 - $45,000			3	10.0 %
$46,000 - $50,000			2	6.6 %
$51,000 - Upper Income			10	33.3 %
No Response(s)			0	0.0 %
		Totals	30	100%

APPENDIX E: LIKER-TYPE SCALE RESULTS

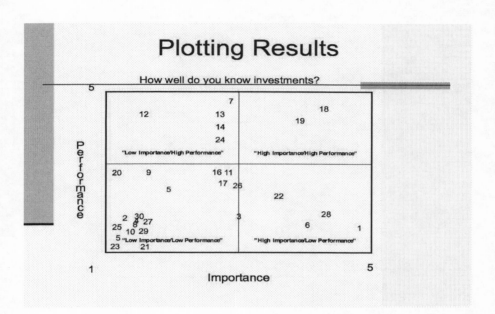

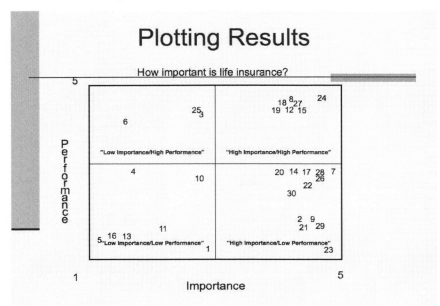

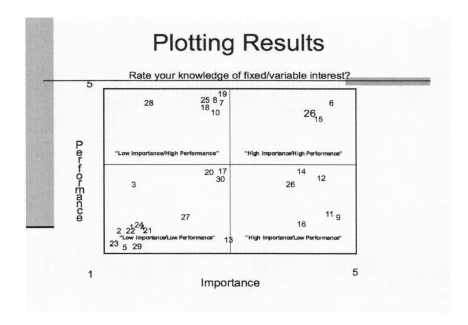

Plotting Results

How important is your credit score?

Performance

5

"Low Importance/High Performance"

"High Importance/High Performance"

24

15
8 3 6
16 17
18 12
28
27 21 25 9 14
22 9 13 26 2 11
23 23 30 5 1

10

"Low Importance/Low Performance"

"High Importance/Low Performance"

4   19

1   Importance   5

About the Author

Dr. Joseph M. Blake Jr. is an Investment Advisor Representative, with a company based out of Duluth, Georgia. He is also, founder of BlakeMediaLLC a digital marketing organization.

Married to his wife of 21 years the wonderful Corina Blake together we have a blended family four amazing Adult children. Jessica, Joe III, Trayvone and Chervonda with 4.5 Grandchildren; the source of our motivation.

Dr. Blake served thirteen years in the United States Air Force where he was decorated with two Achievement Medals for performance and honored with a Commendation Medal for meritorious service.

He holds a Bachelor of Science degree in Business Management, a Master of Arts degree in Organizational Management, and a Doctor of Management in Organizational Leadership degree from the University of Phoenix. Dr. Blake completed his groundbreaking research in 2013 entitled, "Financial Literacy's Influence on Faith-Based Epistemology: A Case Study of Arizona Church Members."

The insights from this research led Dr. Blake to create an Actionable Financial Literacy Decision Model (AFDM), a design that helps organizations, their members, and individuals maximize their full financial potential. In fact, an article based on his research received "The Distinguished Paper Award" at the Mustang Journals International Academic Conference held in Las Vegas, NV on Feb 6, 2014.

Dr. Blake began his venture as an Investment Advisor Representative in February 1994 (25 years Ago). As an Advisor, he cultivated more than $3.4 Million in assets under management combining 450 accounts. While holding Licenses: Life, Securities (Series 6, 63, & 65), 401(k), Investment Advisor, Variable Annuities, Indexed Annuities, Fixed Annuities, Long Term Care (LTC), Debt Watcher's, Legal Shield, and Auto & Home Ins. (Referral).